10 Foundational Elements of Intentional Transformation

Mack Story

ISBN-10: 1539104443
ISBN-13: 978-1539104445

DEDICATION

To those with the courage to press the reset button and
move beyond their current circumstances in order
to transform themselves into the person
they were destined to be.

CONTENTS

ACKNOWLEDGMENTS

I would like to recognize those who have a desire to help others become the best version of themselves. You are making a difference in the lives of others who will make a difference in the lives of others. I wish there were more of you.

I will always be grateful to my wife, Ria, for the positive influence she has been in my life. She has inspired much of my transformation while experiencing her own.

INTRODUCTION

"What distinguishes winners from losers is that winners concentrate at all times on what they can do, not what they can't do." ~ Bob Butera

People who have known me since I was a teenager often want to know *how* I transformed myself. In the past, I drank alcohol, partied, had a short-temper, was very reactive, narcissistic, and blamed others for my circumstances. Today, I help develop leaders and their teams. I speak to thousands from the stage each year with a heavy focus on personal growth and leadership.

How did I transform myself? The short answer: I simply decided I wanted to be a better person. Then, I started making better choices and became a better person.

The long answer to the question of *how* I transformed myself is found on the remaining pages of this book.

The first thing I often tell people I haven't seen for many years is, *"The person you knew in the past doesn't live here anymore. He moved out years ago."* Actually, he didn't move out. I kicked him out because he was holding me back.

As you begin your journey through this material, you must understand this book is based on what I call the *10 Foundational Elements of Intentional Transformation.* Each *"layer"* of the foundation is supported by those layers that come before it. The book is divided into 10 sections, one for each of the foundational layers of transformation.

Each section will have three chapters. The first two chapters of each section are intended to introduce a specific foundational layer and teach you the related fundamental leadership principles you must apply as you move forward with your intentional transformation. The third chapter in each section is where I pull back the curtain on my life a bit and share some of my personal stories of transformation. You will see where I failed, where I struggled, and where I eventually succeeded.

The success stories aren't meant to impress you. I share them to motivate and inspire you to move yourself to the next level and beyond. My story is simply that: my story. It is what it is. I *don't* think I'm special. I *don't* think I'm better than *anyone* else. I *do* think I'm *different* than *everyone* else, and *so are you*. We are all unique individuals shaped by all of our unique life experiences. We choose many of our experiences. But, many of our experiences choose us. Life happens.

My wife, Ria, has experienced an amazing transformation of her own after experiencing seven years of extreme sexual abuse at the hands of her father and others from age 12-19. Ria says, *"Transparency is the purest form of truth."* I agree. I also believe *transparency is telling the truth when you don't have to simply because you want to*. When sharing my supporting stories, my intent is to be transparent.

Note: Ria shared her story in three of her books, Ria's Story from Ashes to Beauty, Beyond Bound and Broken: A Journey of Healing and Resilience, and Bridges Out of the Past: A Survivor's Lessons on Resilience. They detail her unimaginable experiences and how she moved beyond surviving and began thriving. More information on her books can be found in the back of this one.

There are many others, like Ria, who have overcome much more than I have and experienced a much more significant transformation than I have. My story is not their story. I can't tell their story. I can only tell mine. All of us who have experienced true transformation have one thing in common. We had to apply the *10 Foundational Elements of Intentional Transformation* in order to make it happen. It doesn't mean we read a book about it and did it. It most likely means we learned the hard way through trial and error. There are no shortcuts.

However, you can intentionally accelerate your transformation with knowledge, understanding, and focused application of the right principles at the right time. This material will build upon itself as you make your way through it. It will be much more meaningful if read at least twice because the layers above add meaning to the layers below. Reflection and re-reading will greatly enhance your ability to understand and intentionally apply these principles of transformation.

Make this book a tool and a resource. Mark it up. Fold the pages. Highlight and underline key points. DON'T GIVE IT AWAY! If you think someone else will get value from it, that's great. Invest in them and purchase a copy for them as a gift, so they can also mark it up and use it as a resource of their own.

My intent is to ENCOURAGE, ENGAGE, and EMPOWER you as you become more focused and intentional about moving from where you are to where you want to be as you create the life you want. You can and will find yourself struggling in some areas while experiencing great success in other areas. That's normal.

Your ability to effectively move from where you are to where you want to be in any area of your life will be determined by your ability to transform your thinking relative to that area of your life. When it comes to true transformation, if you don't go within, you will go without. *You* are the key to your success.

"If you truly want to initiate a change that will redirect your life and unleash your potential, focus on transforming yourself." ~ Mack Story

SECTION 1

THOUGHT IS THE FOUNDATION OF CHOICE

1

THOUGHT IS THE FOUNDATION OF CHOICE

WHAT YOU THINK DETERMINES WHAT YOU DO

"The outer world of circumstance shapes itself to the inner world of thought." ~ James Allen

If you already knew what you needed to know, you would already be where you want to go. Until you change what you think, you will not change what you do.

Your conscious thoughts are real but only in y*our* mind. Your thoughts will lead to other private thoughts and subconscious feelings or emotions. Once you act on your thoughts and feelings, they are translated to the world as choices when they begin to shape your life.

You first make your choices. Then, your choices make you.

The Choice Formula:
Thought + Emotion + Action = Choice

Thought – something we are consciously aware of in our mind

Emotion – something we subconsciously feel based on our thoughts

Action – something we do based on our thoughts and emotions

Your choices flow from your thoughts. The quality of the choices depends on the quality of the thoughts. There is no conscious choice without conscious thought.

Think of what your home looks like or think of your favorite car. Not only can you choose your thoughts, but as you just experienced in this simple exercise, it is very easy for others to influence your thoughts. This is where our real problems start. Far too often, we accept bad influence instead of rejecting it and using our own reasoning to positively influence our thoughts.

James Allen in his book, *As a Man Thinketh*, wrote, *"Our mind may be likened to a garden, which may be intelligently cultivated or allowed to run wild; but whether cultivated or neglected, it must, and will, bring forth. If no useful seeds are put into it, then an abundance of useless weed-seeds will fall therein, and will continue to produce their kind."*

Our mind can be prepared to produce great thoughts and choices just as a freshly plowed field is made ready to produce a great crop. Our mind can also be left undeveloped or underdeveloped to produce whatever thoughts it may without any intentional development. But make no mistake, our mind will produce thoughts. Thoughts and choices will flow from our mind whether good or bad, beneficial or harmful. *Sought or not, there will be thought.* Thoughts will sprout from our mind as plants sprout from the earth. Abundantly.

When you garden, you are responsible for planting seeds capable of producing a great crop. Likewise, you are responsible for developing your mind to produce great thoughts and choices beneficial to you and others. Thoughts that will lead you to where you want to be.

You can take another step and work the garden continuously by watering, weeding, and fertilizing to ensure and enhance the quality of the crop. You can go farther in the development of your mind by associating with people who want to help you by choosing to remove bad habits and toxic people from your life, by intentionally studying positive people, by reading positive books, and by making positive choices.

One very powerful life and death choice is self-talk, *thoughts* you have about yourself and others. Self-talk is far more destructive than what others say to you or about you. Why? Because you are *always* listening to yourself.

People take their lives every day because of their own self-talk, not what others are saying. Sometimes they are not talking to others at all. Their own thoughts have brought them to the point of feeling worthless, helpless, and most often, hopeless. They have convinced themselves there is no reason to continue living.

These people no longer have hope and have given up. When you don't have hope, you must get it from others. You must connect with positive people, be with them, and talk with them. You must borrow their belief in you. They can and will lift you up. If the people you are around don't lift you up, you are around the wrong people. The right people will *always* give you hope and lift you up.

There are endless examples of self-talk (thought) being detrimental to our well-being. You can choose your thoughts and change your thoughts. When you do, you begin to change your habits, your circumstances, and ultimately, your life.

"We imagine that thought can be kept secret, but it cannot; it rapidly crystallizes into habit, and habit solidifies into circumstance." ~ James Allen

2

THOUGHTS ARE BASED ON VALUES

HIGH IMPACT VALUES LEAD TO
HIGH IMPACT THOUGHTS

*"I cannot teach anybody anything,
I can only make them think." ~ Socrates*

Ultimately, you choose your results when you choose your values. *Your values are the foundation for your results.*

Your values influence your thoughts, which influence your feelings, which influence your actions, which *determine* your results. Dramatically different values will always lead to dramatically different results.

V. Gilbert Beers had this to say about values, *"A person of integrity is one who has established a system of values against which all of life is judged."*

Everyone has values. They can be good or bad. You categorize them as good or bad by asking, *"Are my values in alignment with natural laws and principles?"* Natural laws and principles are timeless. Every human understands them regardless of age, race, religion, gender, etc. Fairness is a great example. No one ever taught you the thousands of ways you can be treated unfairly. However, you know when it happens because you *feel* it.

You came fully loaded with the innate ability to understand right and wrong. And, you also came fully loaded with free will, the ability to choose to adhere to natural laws and principles or to go completely against them. You have an internal *"map"* with street lights along the path you should take, but you also have the awareness and ability to see and travel the dimly lit and dark paths you should avoid.

Do you *value* accepting responsibility or transferring responsibility? When you look through the window and blame others, you are transferring responsibility. Statements like *"You make me so mad!"* are made by those who choose to blame and transfer responsibility. When you look in the mirror to find the solution to your problems, you are accepting responsibility. Statements like *"How was this my fault?"* and *"What could I have done differently?"* are made by those who choose to reflect on and accept responsibility for the situation.

Your values are the foundation upon which you base your thoughts. My book, *10 Values of High Impact Leaders,* details 10 key values everyone should work to master because those values will have a tremendous impact on one's ability to positively influence others. The more influence you have, the more options you will have. Since influence is very dynamic and complex, the more values you have been able to internalize and utilize synergistically together, the more effective you will be and the more influence you will have. So, where do you start?

There is a story of a tourist who paused for a rest in a small town in the mountains. He went over to an old man sitting on a bench in front of the only store in town and inquired, *"Friend, can you tell me something this town is noted for?"*

"Well," replied the old man, *"I don't rightly know except it's the starting point to the world. You can start here and go anywhere you want."*

That's a great little story. We are all at *"the starting point to the world."* We can start where we are and go anywhere.

We can expand our influence 360° in all directions by simply starting in the center and expanding ourselves.

Consider the illustration below. Imagine you are standing in the center. You can make a high impact. However, it will not happen by accident. You *must* become *intentional.* You must *live with purpose* while *focusing on your performance* as you *unleash your potential.*

Why we do what we do is about our *purpose.* **How** we do what we do is about our *performance.* **What** we do will unleash our *potential.* Where these three components overlap, you will achieve a **HIGH IMPACT**.

"The values that form the basis for your True North are derived from your beliefs and convictions. In defining your values, you must decide what is most important in your life. Is it maintaining your integrity, making a difference, helping other people, or devoting yourself to family? There is no one right set of values. Only you can decide the question of your values." ~ Bill George

3

THE THOUGHT THAT CHANGED MY LIFE

IN ORDER TO TRANSFORM YOURSELF, YOU MUST FIRST BE ABLE TO LEAD YOURSELF

"Nothing splendid has ever been achieved except by those who dared believe that something inside themselves was superior to circumstance."
~ Bruce Barton

I'll never forget the first time I heard Stephen R. Covey say 14 words that would change the rest of my life. He said, *"Between stimulus and response, we have the ability to pause and choose our response."* As simple as these words sound today, they were profound at that moment. I had never intentionally thought about what he had just taught me.

The year was 2008. I had recently resigned from 20 years in the corporate world to start my own process improvement (Lean Manufacturing) consulting business. At the time, I was listening to a one hour audio featuring the highlights of Covey's book, *The 7 Habits of Highly Effective People*. I didn't find out there was a book by the same title until many months later. I would also later learn the entire audio book was approximately 13 hours.

One hour only scratched the surface. However, that was exactly what I needed to get me going, not too much at the start, just a taste of what could be. This book is meant to scratch the surface in the same way. It's meant to stir your thoughts, motivate you to action, and inspire you along the path of transformation.

Many of us need to experience a character-based transformation. Unfortunately, most of us don't know it. I didn't know it until 2008. I thought I was a great person.

We naturally tend to spend more time looking out the window judging others instead of looking in the mirror judging ourselves. Transformation requires a lot of time intentionally looking in the mirror as we reflect on who we really are. For most of us, our intentional growth focuses on developing our competency (what we know) and very little, if any, intentional effort is put into developing our character (who we are).

Well-developed character *always* serves as a multiplier of our competency.

During our lifetime, most of us only experience accidental character growth. There aren't near as many among us who will experience a real, intentional character transformation. Transformation at the core, at the character level, does not happen by accident. It happens by choice. A choice to change your values followed by a lifetime of choices to align your behavior with timeless, tested, proven, natural laws and values.

When I first heard Covey speak about stimulus and response, I actually paused the audio and thought about what he was saying. Fortunately for me, I was paying attention, and those powerful words didn't go unnoticed. It was actually as if he had reached out of my car stereo and literally shook me to get my attention while saying, *"Listen to me, son. I'm talking to you!"*

At the time, I needed to hear those words for many reasons, some of which I wouldn't understand until much later into my transformational journey. The key for me at that moment was how they effortlessly *stuck* in my mind. They resonated with me at the core. They made a lot of sense. I still think about them, say them to myself, and use the principle found in them daily. That day in 2008, I actually pressed rewind on my audio player and listened, paused, and reflected on his words many times before I let the audio continue.

Until I was exposed to the formal principles of character-based leadership I started learning from Covey, I didn't think very intentionally about my character at all. I had been experiencing non-stop growth throughout my entire life. In my mind, I had been very successful.

Success is a relative term. To most, success means a good job, a good and steady income, a nice home, and a nice life. To a few, those who have highly developed character, success means mastery of self. Only when we have mastered self are we truly successful. Then, everything else in life becomes a bonus. We don't simply live our life. We design, build, and create our life on a foundation of solid well-developed character.

I didn't experience transformation in my life until I was 42. My character growth had always been accidental. If you would have spoken to me before then, I would have told you I was successful. I would have felt proud of what I had accomplished. However, after hearing those words, my *thoughts* began to change. My *thoughts* began to move me away from the window and closer to the mirror.

I believed every word Covey had said. I also believed *I could change myself.* For the first time, I began to imagine what would change if I changed my thoughts.

"All that a man achieves or fails to achieve is the direct result of his thoughts." ~ James Allen

SECTION 2

CHOICE IS THE FOUNDATION OF VISION

4

CHOICE IS THE FOUNDATION OF VISION

IF YOU DON'T KNOW WHERE YOU'RE GOING, YOU'LL END UP SOMEWHERE ELSE

"Destiny is not a matter of chance, but a matter of choice. It is not a thing to be waited for but is a thing to be achieved." ~ William Jennings Bryan

There is no conscious action without conscious thought. You can turn your potential into your reality. The quality of your *choices* depends on the quality of your thoughts. When is the last time you spent 10 minutes per day for 90 consecutive days thinking about where you want to be and how you're going to get there? Doing so is simply a *choice* you can make.

Most people haven't spent one day thinking intentionally for 10 minutes about where they want to be and how they are going to get there. Far too many people get trapped in a never ending cycle of doing the same thing day in and day out while hoping, wishing, and praying for different results. This makes absolutely no sense when you *actually* think about it. But, most people *don't* think about it.

You are responsible for *choosing* to move yourself forward. Until you *choose* to realize this simple fact, you will be at the mercy of society. And, society doesn't have a lot planned for you. Once you make the *choice* to become responsible you have positioned yourself to make some amazing things happen.

As Dee Ann Turner stated so simply, *"Wise choices in the beginning provide a better chance of success in the end."* When you make the *choice* to respond to everything based on internalized values that are timeless, tested, and have been proven across generations, you are prepared to launch yourself to the next level and beyond.

When it comes to creating a compelling vision for yourself, you must intentionally tap into your passion and purpose to begin to think of what could be. Too many people chase money instead of things that make them happy. As a result, they get neither. You will be the happiest when you're earning a living doing something you are passionate about and that interests you. Odds are, you will also earn more money over a lifetime doing it. And if you don't, it won't matter because you'll be happy simply because you're doing what you love.

Developing a vision, big or small, is a *choice*. We must think on purpose about our purpose. Most people are far removed from their purpose. When asked what their purpose is, most don't have an answer. However, the most common answer is, *"I don't know."* Or, *"I've never really thought about it."*

If you are serious about creating the life you want instead of continuing to live the life you have accepted, it's time to *choose* to think about your purpose. Once you know who you are and who you want to become and once you know where you are and where you want to be, you can begin your transformation. Transformation is a choice that only responsible people can and will make.

Transformation turns vision into reality. You must intentionally *choose* to dream of what is possible. You must *choose* to let your imagination run wild. Who do you want to become? What do you want to do? Where do you want to go? When do you want to go? Don't ask, *"Can I do it?"* Ask, *"Is it possible?"* Think, *"How can I make it happen?"* and *"When can I make it happen?"* Then, follow up with the most important question of all, *"What's stopping me from making it happen?"*

When you ask these questions, don't look out the window for excuses. An effective vision taps into your strengths not your weaknesses. Look into the mirror, *choose* to be responsible, and find a way to make it happen. You are exactly where you're supposed to be based on every choice you've made leading up to this moment.

Will things outside of your control happen to you? Absolutely…until the day you die. Those things are important and will influence you along your journey. However, there's something much more important than what happens to you.

The most important thing is your response to what happens to you. You don't always get to choose what happens to you. But, you will *always* get to *choose your response* to what happens to you. Your response to what happens will determine much, but not all, of what happens to you in the future.

Regardless of what has happened to you or what will happen to you in the future, the *choices* you make daily will *always* shape your future. When you *choose* to intentionally create a vision for your future, you're aligned to make the *choices* that will create that future. Things will happen outside of your control. When they do, you simply regroup, reevaluate the situation, look forward, make the necessary adjustments, and continue creating your future.

"A man's environment is a merciless mirror of him as a human being." ~ Earl Nightingale

5

CHOICES CREATE THE FUTURE

WHAT WE CHOOSE TO DO
TODAY WILL DETERMINE WHAT
WE GET TO DO TOMORROW

"Show me someone who is humble enough to accept and take responsibility for his or her circumstances and courageous enough to take whatever initiative is necessary to creatively work his or her way through or around these challenges, and I'll show you the supreme power of choice." ~ Stephen R. Covey

When you *choose* to accept responsibility for your future, you will be able to define your future.

Apply what is on these pages, and you will be amazed at the future you will create. A future you can't begin to imagine now. There are opportunities for you right now that you can't see. You must start preparing for those opportunities without knowing what they are. You must *trust they are there* and begin moving toward them.

It's much like taking a trip in a car at night. You can't see very much in the dark. If you want to see ahead in the dark, you must first turn on the lights. Then, if you want to see farther ahead, you must start moving slowly in the direction you think you want to go. As you move, you will begin to see what was previously unseen.

Your growth toward a better and preferred future is exactly the same. You're holding in your hand a way forward, if you'll turn the light on (take responsibility) and

18

start moving forward toward your vision (growth). As Henry Cloud says, *"If you have already been trying hard, maybe trying harder is not the way. Try different."*

If you don't choose to create your future, the cumulative choices of society will determine your future. You can choose to navigate your way to your destination, or you can refuse to navigate your way to your destination. If you refuse to navigate your way forward, it's like being adrift in the ocean. There's no telling where you'll end up or when you'll get there. In other words, you will be helpless and hopeless.

Unfortunately, that's exactly how many people live their lives. They are where they are because that's where they ended up. By not choosing to be someplace else, they chose to be there. By not choosing to navigate their way forward, they simply drifted into a career or job, and maybe, into a bad relationship. Instead of intentionally creating their future, they accidentally created their future.

Too often, people who are searching in life find what they will settle for and stop looking for what they were searching for. As John G. Miller remarked, *"There's nothing you have to do. We all have the power to make a decision that will direct us to a new destination. Each of us can make a choice that will change our life."*

The future is in you now. Think about that for a moment. Your future really is in you now. That's not a play on words. It's the truth. Your future is defined and refined by the *choices* you make every day. Make a bad *choice*, and you get a less desirable future. Make a good *choice*, and you get a more desirable future. You can easily see you are very much in control of creating your future. You don't have to settle. It's your choice.

You can't predict your future, but *you can create your future*. This is powerful and profound if you have never taken the time to slow down and truly think it out. The thousands of *choices* we make every day of our life, not only shape our life, but they also create our future.

Remember, with only a few exceptions, you're exactly where you're supposed to be based on all of the *choices* you have made leading up to this moment. If you were supposed to be someplace else, you would already be there. You must own the results your *choices* have produced. James Allen said it best, *"We are anxious to improve our circumstances but unwilling to improve ourselves. We therefore remain bound."*

Until you own that you're responsible, you're being irresponsible. That's why those blaming others for their circumstances can't improve their circumstances.

The thought process of blaming someone else for your circumstances has a zero chance of making anything in your life better. Many people wake up and live out this model from start to finish every day.

Why? Because when we blame others, we don't have to do anything. We truly believe someone else is responsible, and think they should do everything. But, when we take the blame, we are 100% responsible. Now, *we* must do everything.

Most people take the easy way out and blame others for their circumstances. It takes a higher level of character development to accept responsibility for your circumstances and make changes when necessary. Don't fear change. Embrace change. Then, learn to leverage change for greater benefit.

Don't be fearful. Be hopeful. It's a choice.

"May your choices reflect your hopes, not your fears."
~ Nelson Mandela

6

ONE OF MANY BAD CHOICES

OUR CHOICES ARE THE INK WE USE TO WRITE OUR STORY. CHOOSE WISELY.

"Choices always come with consequences. Choosing wisely brings the consequences we want in life. Choosing poorly will bring the consequences we don't want in life." ~ Ria Story

As I mentioned previously, transparency is telling the truth when we don't have to simply because we want to. That's what I'm about to do in this chapter. It's one thing to talk about the value of being transparent. It's another thing to actually be transparent. However, transparency is powerful relative to building credibility and trust.

Transparency is a tool high impact leaders use to leverage their influence with others. Being transparent at the right time for the right reason can boost our influence with others. Being transparent can motivate others to take action. Being transparent can influence others to intentionally reflect on their choices and inspire them to make changes to improve their lives.

The timing is right to share this very personal story of failure. The timing in my life is right, and the timing in this book is right. I've heard it said, *"We learn the most when others share about their failure, not about their success."* I agree.

If we choose the right response after making a bad choice, we can turn a bad choice into an amazing learning experience. In other words, bad choices can be leveraged to produce good results and to create a better future. Reflection allows us to leverage past experiences.

May 17th, 2012 was a Thursday. I remember it well. I was traveling on business supporting a client near Dallas, Texas. That afternoon, I had finished leading a very successful week long process improvement event with an amazing cross-functional team. The next morning the team would be making a final presentation and sharing their accomplishments with their leaders, so my work was already done.

I was staying at a hotel near a large lake. Thursday evening after an exciting week of making things happen, I went to the hotel, took a shower, and went out for a nice dinner at one of the restaurants located near the lake. During the summer, there was a *"Concert on the Harbor"* on Thursday nights and thousands of people would come to the area to enjoy the event.

I always enjoyed having dinner at a great little Cajun restaurant by the harbor. I would sit at the bar, make some new friends, have a great meal, and have a few of my favorite adult beverages. No big deal. I had done it many times on many Thursdays for many years.

I was 42 years old at the time. I had started drinking alcohol at an early age in high school when I was only 15 years old. Until that day in May 2012, the only *major* alcohol related problem I had experienced was a DUI many years before when I was 21 years old. I stopped drinking alcohol for a year or so after that, but eventually started back.

That night in Texas, I made some new friends who invited me to join them after dinner for the concert. Several hours, many laughs, and many more drinks later, I was walking back to my hotel when I was approached by a police officer. Officer Garcia had been providing security at the concert near our location. He and I had several friendly conversations during the evening, so he already knew I had been drinking. He had been watching.

After he asked me a few questions about the number of drinks I had consumed, he made the decision to arrest me for public intoxication. I realized I was about to pay the price for the bad choices *I had made* that evening.

There wasn't a taxi service in this small town, so I had three choices to avoid driving under the influence: don't drink (too late), ride with someone else (not an option), or walk to the hotel (it was only a few blocks away). I chose to walk to prevent the possibility of a DUI. The possibility of being arrested for walking back to my hotel intoxicated never entered my mind.

Choosing to drink was a bad choice. However, I have made the right choice every day since. I haven't drank a drop of alcohol since and never will again.

The very next day, I immediately leveraged the bad choice to create a good outcome. By sharing it on these pages with you, I'm leveraging the bad choice once again for another good outcome. The good I have leveraged over the years from this bad choice has *far* outweighed the bad that came from it.

Change is the foundation of transformation. We can change without transforming, but we can't transform without changing. I didn't simply decide to make a change after the bad choice. I chose to start my transformation on May 18th, 2012.

Nearly everything we allow into our life or keep out of our life is a choice. We either ask for it by choosing it or deny it by refusing it.

"Who you are tomorrow is determined by the choices you make today." ~ Ria Story

SECTION 3

VISION IS THE FOUNDATION OF HOPE

7

VISION IS THE FOUNDATION OF HOPE

WHAT WE CHOOSE TO IMAGINE WILL MAKE US FEEL FEARFUL OR HOPEFUL

"There are three requirements for humans to act: 1) dissatisfaction with the present state of affairs, 2) a vision of a better state, and 3) belief that we can reach that better state. When just one of the requirements is missing, people will not act." ~ Ludwig von Mises

Several years ago, I discovered a rather odd but impactful story illustrating how vision can create hope. An experiment was performed with laboratory rats to measure their motivation to survive under different circumstances.

Scientists would drop a rat into a jar of water that had been placed in total darkness (no vision) and time how long the it would continue swimming before it gave up (hopeless) and allowed itself to drown. The scientists discovered the rats would usually survive approximately three minutes in the dark without hope.

Next, the scientists dropped other rats individually into the same type of jar, but instead of placing them in total darkness (no vision/no hope), they allowed a ray of light (hope) to shine in.

Under those circumstances, the rat kept swimming for 36 hours with the ray of light (hope). That's 720 times longer than those trying to survive in the dark with no vision and no hope.

Because the rats could see (vision), they continued to have hope. If this is true for a rat, imagine the amount of hope a strong and powerful personal vision will provide you. You are much more capable of imagining and reasoning yourself into a brighter future, one filled with light instead of darkness.

Once you have a clearly defined vision, you must again ask yourself, *"Is it possible my vision can become my reality?"* You may not be able to tell yourself with integrity you can do it. If not, don't lie to yourself. However, don't concern yourself with trying to decide if you can or can't do it. That's not important.

What is important is your belief that *it is possible*. Knowing it's possible will provide you with the hope you need to turn your vision into your reality.

You should also seek reinforcement from those who believe in you and your mission. Others who believe in you will also reinforce your belief that your vision is possible. Look for those who will support you and avoid those who won't.

Most often, people you don't know can help you the most. How can someone you don't know help you the most? Because they have written books, made audios, and made videos to help people just like you.

You're reading a book right now, most likely written by someone you don't know, who wants to help you move forward. Someone who believes in you and your vision. Reading books written by people who have done what you want to do or by people who are doing what you want to do, allows you to get into some of the greatest minds with the most valuable insight.

Whatever you do, don't make the common mistake of asking your friends and relatives to validate your vision. Unless they have done what you want to do or are doing what you want to do, they are not likely to provide meaningful support. Instead, they will usually question your ability, provide plenty of reasons it can't or won't happen, and place doubt in your mind.

These people are not necessarily bad people. They simply haven't been where you've been and don't want to go where you're going. If you decide to climb to the top of Mt. Everest, you will obviously want to seek support, guidance, and direction from someone who has already been to the top (a tour guide). You will not want to seek support, guidance, and direction from someone who has only booked trips for people who want to climb to the top (a travel agent). This simple principle applies in all areas related to turning your vision into reality.

Viktor Frankl made this wise observation, *"Everyone has his own specific vocation or mission in life. Everyone must carry out a concrete assignment that demands fulfillment. Therein he cannot be replaced, nor can his life be repeated. Thus everyone's task is as unique as his specific opportunity to implement it."* You are unique. Your vision is unique. Some may not understand. That's okay. Make it happen anyway.

Without vision, your hope will fade into darkness as it did with the rats. But with vision, your hope remains, giving you a reason to *keep swimming*. You must maintain hope that your vision will become your reality.

Knowing it is possible will give you hope. Having faith in your vision will give you hope. Having people believe in you and your vision will give you hope. Knowing others have done what you want to do will give you hope.

"Cherish your vision and your dreams as they are the children of your soul, the blueprints of your ultimate achievements." ~ Napoleon Hill

8

VISION PROVIDES DIRECTION

KNOWING WHERE WE'RE GOING
ALLOWS US TO CHART THE COURSE

"Clarity of vision will compensate for uncertainty in planning. If you are unclear about the destination of the journey, even the most sophisticated, well-thought-through strategy is useless. Pencil in your plans. Etch the vision in stone." ~ Andy Stanley

When your vision flows from your passion and purpose, you will find clarity and will become a highly effective and highly influential individual. You will begin to live a much more fulfilling and rewarding life. You will live a life most people will never experience, but many will dream about.

In order to fully leverage your passion to increase your influence, you must use it to find, reveal, and refine your *why* – your purpose. You must follow your passion to find your purpose. Discovering your purpose doesn't happen accidentally as you go through life. It happens intentionally as you grow through life. Finding your purpose sounds simple, but it's not. It requires a lot of discipline, stretching, risk taking, determination, and searching without settling.

Unfortunately, many people will go to their grave never discovering their *why*. Instead, they will choose to settle for mediocrity instead of greatness. Why would anyone settle for mediocrity when they could become exceptional? It's simple. Very little effort is required to be mediocre. However, to become exceptional, an extraordinary and continuous effort will be required. It takes a lot of work to continually grow and develop yourself, but it's worth it.

When you align your purpose with your vision you know you're heading in the right direction. A vision without a purpose is like having a map but no idea where you want to go. If you don't know where you want to go, a map will not be of any use to you. Actually, if you don't know where you're going, you don't need a map.

This simple illustration explains why most people haven't defined a detailed vision for themselves. They don't know where they're going. They haven't fully accepted responsibility for developing their own personal vision. If they don't know where they're going and don't care where they're going, why do they need to see (create a vison for themselves)? They don't, and they won't.

Many people are not on a mission. They are not on a journey. They have no vision. They are wandering aimlessly through life waiting on something good to happen, waiting on life to give them a break, waiting to retire, and ultimately, waiting to die. It sounds a bit harsh. But, it's the choice many people make consciously or unconsciously. That is not living. That is loafing.

William Barclay made a powerful statement when he said, *"There are two great days in a person's life – the day you are born and the day you discover why."* Everyone experiences the first day – the day we are born. It's hard to miss that one. However, very few experience the second day. Very few of us ever discover *why* we were born. This book will challenge you to discover *your* why. Or, if you're already well on your way to discovering your why, it will help you *leverage* your why.

No matter your passion and purpose, you must be able to influence people in order to add value to them and be valued by them. You must be able to influence them to voluntarily follow you. You must define and refine your vision in order to get closer to living the life you want instead of living the one you've been given. However, your ability to influence other people will determine where you're able to go and when you're able to go.

Everything in your life will rise and fall based on the amount of influence you're able to create with others. Your vision will help you identify who you need to influence. Your values, character, and competency will determine if you're actually able to influence them. Your vision will help you identify what you need to learn in order to be able to influence others along your journey.

Your vision will also help you discover who you need to become on the inside in order to influence the right people on the outside. Your vision will serve as your roadmap for your intentional growth journey.

The most important thing your vision will reveal is who you need to become and what you need to know. When it comes to vision, your character will take you most of the way. And, your competency will take you the rest of the way.

Many people don't want to create a vision for their life because they already know they are unwilling to put in the work. Without action, your vision will be only a dream.

"Vision is not enough. It must be combined with venture. It is not enough to stare up the steps; we must step up the stairs." ~ Vaclav Havel

9

VISION ALLOWS FOCUS

CHANGE IS OFTEN TEMPORARY, BUT TRANSFORMATION IS USUALLY PERMANENT

"Nothing is impossible, if only your
will power is strong enough." ~ Bruce Barton

When I was arrested in Texas because I chose to drink alcohol and walk back to my hotel along a public street, I also chose the related consequences. It wasn't my new friend's fault for inviting me to have drinks. It wasn't the fault of the city for not having a taxi service. It wasn't the arresting officer's fault. It was my fault for choosing to drink alcohol.

If I hadn't drank alcohol that night, none of the other things would have happened. I wouldn't have been arrested for any type of alcohol related offense if I was 100% sober. That much was very clear to me on May 18th, 2012. I knew I was responsible for my choices.

As Covey stated so well, *"Between stimulus and response, we have the ability to pause and choose our response."* Something happened (stimulus): I had achieved great results with the team and was feeling really good about the success. Then, I chose my response (without pausing): I went out for dinner and drinks to celebrate because I was excited about what we had accomplished together.

Covey also said, *"Proactive people respond based on values in alignment with natural laws and principles, and reactive people respond based on feelings."*

That Thursday night in 2012, I didn't respond based on values. Or, maybe I did because I valued having a good time, and I valued having a few drinks. But, there's no doubt I absolutely responded based on feelings. I felt good and wanted to feel better by going out and having a few drinks to celebrate.

After four years of reading, studying, applying, and teaching leadership, I still struggled *at times* to make good choices. I was making much better choices in some areas of my life while still making bad choices in other areas of my life. I didn't know at the time that some of those choices were holding me back.

Once we learn we have the freedom to choose our response in any situation, we must accept responsibility. I had figured that much out. What happened in Texas was my fault. Luckily, after a night in jail, all I had to do was pay several hundred dollars in fines, stay out of trouble for the next 90 days, and the offense would not appear on my record. That was easy enough.

To the rest of the world, it would be as if it never happened. The *"old"* Mack would have been happy about that and continued doing what he had been doing. I would have thought I had gotten away without a scratch one more time. But, a *"new"* Mack was emerging after four years of daily reading and application of leadership principles. It had changed me. For me, whether it's on my record or not, it did happen. And, it happened because of my bad choice. I realized I wasn't leading myself well.

My focus had been on making small changes. I had not been focused on a big transformation. Changing is easy. You simply do *some* things differently. Transformation is hard. You must become a *totally* different person.

The other principle I learned from Covey is related to vision. He described it as the habit of personal leadership. He said it simply, *"Begin with the end in mind."*

This principle explains the root cause of my bad choice that night. I knew I was responsible and was okay with making the choice to have drinks. But, I didn't truly know where I was headed in life. Therefore, my bad choice wasn't really too bad in that context. The night spent in jail helped give me the clarity I needed. That was a huge positive, not a negative.

The clarity didn't come from simply being in jail for 12 hours. In 1987, I spent three months at Parris Island, South Carolina going through the United States Marine Corps boot camp. That experience made most other things in life seem like a walk in the park. The clarity came because for the first time I realized my vision for the future was to have a career in professional leadership development.

I also realized if I continued to make the same types of choices it would never happen at the level I envisioned myself being at in the future. I had learned enough to know my character and integrity would be the key to climbing my way to the top in the professional leadership industry. I had to transform who I was and how I thought to ensure I would *always* make better choices. I chose to align my values with natural laws and principles.

Changing wouldn't be enough. I needed to transform.

"What we fear doing most is usually what we most need to do." ~ Tim Ferriss

SECTION 4

HOPE IS THE FOUNDATION OF SACRIFICE

10

HOPE IS THE FOUNDATION OF SACRIFICE

WHEN THERE IS HOPE FOR THE FUTURE, THERE IS MEANING IN THE SACRIFICE

"There are no hopeless situations; there are only men and women who have grown hopeless about them."
~ Marshal Ferdinand Foch

Without hope, there will be no sacrifice. When you can see the potential for a better future and you believe it is possible, you develop hope. When there's hope for a better future, you are more likely to pay a price (sacrifice) to turn that preferred future into your reality.

Vision provides hope, and hope provides a reason to make sacrifices. For example, you may be able to see (vision) how a college degree will help you get a job in a field that interests you. The vision of getting the degree and being paid to do what you *want to do* instead of continuing to do what you *have to do* gives you hope for a better future.

Because you have hope for a better future, you will be more likely to sacrifice your resources, such as time, money, and activities, to do what is required to earn the degree you *feel* you need. However, if you don't *feel* having the degree will help, there will be no hope and no sacrifice. Without the sacrifice, you will not get the degree or, most likely, the job. Hope is a feeling.

Michael Hyatt got it right when he said, *"You can either accept reality as it is or create it as you wish it to be."* Those without hope simply accept reality as it is. Those with hope are positioned to create it as they wish it to be.

Without hope, you will be at the mercy of society. You will get what others want you to have when they want you to have it. Life does not have to be that way. As long as you are able to make choices, you will be able to change your circumstances. However, very little will change without hope for a better future.

Hope can inspire you from within to make the necessary sacrifices. When you have hope, you believe things will be better. When you consider your vision, you look at where you are and compare it to where you want to be. You don't hope for things to get worse. You hope for things to get better.

If you believe strongly enough in yourself and your vision (hope), you will have the strength and desire to make the many sacrifices needed to transform your vision into your reality. Hope allows you to look in the mirror, accept responsibility, and ask, *"What can I do?" "What should I do?"* And, *"When should I do it?"*

If you don't believe strongly enough in yourself and your vision (hopeless), you will not have the strength or desire to make the many sacrifices needed to transform your vision into your reality. Instead of hoping and sacrificing, you begin to wish and wonder. Those wishing and wondering tend to transfer responsibility, look out the window, and say, *"I wish things were better."* and *"I wonder if things will ever change."*

To move closer to your vision, you must first become more hopeful about the possibilities that lie ahead. You may have been through a lot. You may have already overcome a lot. But to move forward, regardless of who you are and where you are, you must continue to have hope for a better future. When you stop having hope, you will stop moving forward.

Sacrifice is giving up something of lesser value now for something of greater value later. Having the vision and foresight to see the greater value is not enough. You must act on that vision. When you give up something, you feel the loss immediately. However, you may not realize the gain until days, weeks, months, or years later.

Hope is powerful and will help inspire you to make the tough choices. If you can't generate hope from within, from your thoughts, or from your faith, there's only one other place to get it, from other people who believe in you. We've all had someone believe in us when we haven't believed in ourselves. Belief from the outside can work miracles on the inside.

If you find yourself hopeless, you must choose to borrow hope from the outside until you develop it on the inside. There are no excuses because we all have the freedom to choose our response in any circumstance. As James Allen stated so well, *"Circumstance does not make the man; it reveals him to himself."*

Do you need hope? Try talking to a friend or family member. Too often, people will say, *"But, I don't have anyone to talk to."* That's an *excuse* to remain hopeless, not a *reason* to remain hopeless. Read a book. Books have given many people hope. Books have transformed many lives. Books have saved lives. If you want to be hopeful, you can be. It's a choice. If you want to be hopeless, you can be. That's also a choice.

"Extraordinary people survive under the most terrible circumstances and then become more extraordinary because of it." ~ Robertson Davies

11

HOPE IS NOT A STRATEGY

HOPE HAS THE POWER TO LAUNCH YOU, BUT HOPE CANNOT DELIVER YOU

"It really is amazing what happens when you recognize the importance of the opportunities ahead of you, accept responsibility for your future, and take positive action." ~ Michael F. Sciortino, Sr.

Hope is not a strategy. However, hope is necessary to develop a strategy. Why? Without hope, you won't be inspired to develop a strategy. Without hope, your vision will never be more than a dream.

You must know and fully understand this truth: *hope is never enough*. Hope is great, but hope is only one layer of the transformational foundation. If you want to create a complete transformation in any area of your life, you must keep adding layers to the foundation.

Remember, there are *10 Foundational Elements of Intentional Transformation*. Each layer will allow you to climb higher and see farther. Each layer must remain in place because it supports the layers above.

Hope simply serves as one layer of the multi-layered foundation that will allow you to add more layers as you move upward and onward. If you keep these layers in place, you will be able to use them to constantly support all areas of your life. Every time you want to be more, do more, have more, accomplish more, or simply make a necessary change in your life for any reason, you must have the necessary foundation in place to support the transformation. Once you understand how each layer is used, you can much more intentionally, effectively, and efficiently use them to support all areas of your life.

This entire book was written to help you navigate your transformational journey. It's a map that will allow you to see what lies ahead. It's a map that reveals the obstacles. It's a map that reveals the most effective and efficient path to transformation.

Like any journey, once you have completed it, you are better equipped to complete it again. You will also be equipped to help others navigate along their path. I have used these foundational elements of transformation many times with great success. I have tested and proven the principles that fill these pages.

At this point in your transformational journey, you must choose to begin leading yourself at a higher level. The most important person you will ever lead is yourself. You must choose to accept full responsibility for making the right choices or the wrong choices as you create your future. Make the right choice, and you get closer to a better future. Make the wrong choice, and you get farther away from what it is you want.

There's a question you need to start asking yourself today. It's a question I will be asking myself regularly for the rest of my life. It's about *"beginning with the end in mind."* It's about taking the right action at the right time for the right reason.

Since I first heard the question, I have never stopped asking it, answering it, acting on it, or sharing it with others. It's the guiding force behind my transformation. This question has allowed me to move from wishing and wondering, to being and doing. It has shaped, and continues to shape, my life.

Every one of us is someplace. However, most of us want to be in a different place. Most of us are uncertain about what to do to move from where we are to where we want to be. The question I'm going to share *assumes you know where you're going*. If you don't know, you need to nail down the answers to the following two sets of questions first. They will help you continue to define and refine your vision.

This first set of questions will establish your *starting point*: *"Who am I?"* And, *"Where am I?"* The second set of questions will establish your *destination*: *"Who do I want to become?"* And, *"Where do I want to be?"*

They also reveal a gap. I call this the *"Success Gap."* The gap between where you are and where you want to be.

Here's the question you need to learn to ask yourself: *"Will what I'm about to do move me in the right direction?"*

This question is packed full of potential just like you and me. The question is important. The answer is more important. But, your actions are most important.

It's actually a very simple concept. Ask yourself the question when you have a choice to make. If the answer is yes, you do it. If the answer is no, you don't do it. *It says easy, but it does hard*. When the answer is yes, and you follow through, you close the gap. When the answer is no, but you do it anyway, you widen the gap.

"When you decide to pursue greatness, you are taking responsibility for your life. This means that you are choosing to accept the consequences of your actions, and to become the agent of your mental, physical, spiritual, and material success. You may not always be able to control what life puts in your path, but I believe you can always control who you are."
~ Les Brown

12

FOR ME, HOPE WAS THE KEY

HOPE ALLOWED ME TO SEE
THROUGH THE DARKNESS

"One of the most common causes of failure is the habit of quitting when one is overtaken by temporary defeat." ~ Napoleon Hill

For some, the bad choice that landed me in jail for a night may not seem like a big deal. Prior to 2008, it wouldn't have been a big deal for me. But, on May 17th, 2012 it was a very dark moment for me. It was as if everything I had been learning about leadership and teaching others about leadership was just for show.

It was obvious to those who knew what had happened; I was teaching one thing and doing another. That is not how you build integrity as a high impact leader. Until that night, I had been learning, teaching, and applying leadership principles. However, my focus was to primarily apply them professionally at work while serving my clients.

As a result, I became much more effective leading my teams. But, I hadn't really considered how my personal choices outside of work could and would impact my ability to lead and influence others professionally.

As odd as it may seem, I'm glad I made the bad choice in Texas on that Thursday night. I'm glad I went to the restaurant, sat at the bar, and ordered a few drinks. I'm glad I connected with the stranger and his friends who sat down beside me. I'm glad I joined them for drinks. I'm glad Officer Garcia did his job on the night of May 17th, 2012. I'm glad I spent the night in jail.

I'm not ashamed it all happened because I was able to learn many lessons from the experience. Today, I believe it was supposed to happen.

Everything that happened that night served as a catalyst for my transformation. Because I began to walk the talk from that moment on, my life has been better and continues to get better. Because I chose to intentionally apply what I had first learned from Covey four years earlier, only positive things came from the bad situation I had created in my life. I used the space between stimulus and response to choose my response based on my values which had better aligned with natural laws and principles because of my four years of reading leadership books that were based on Biblical principles.

At the time, I was agnostic. I didn't give credit to any God for anything that was happening in my life. But, I had been steadily aligning myself with His principles.

When it came to religion, I was basically neutral. I simply didn't know or care to know if there was a God. As I write this in late 2016, it's been a little over four years since I began my transformation. Many amazing things have happened in my life that I couldn't have imagined would happen and never would have believed would happen as I made my way to the jail handcuffed in the back of a police car on the night of May 17th, 2012.

Today, I am a Christian. I accepted Christ at a service with leadership guru, John Maxwell in West Palm Beach, Florida on my 43rd birthday in August 2012. I was baptized by my wife's Grandfather in 2014. In 2015, I read the Bible from cover to cover. I read every word printed on every page, even the glossary. If I was going to be a Christian, I wasn't going to be a Christian who had never read the Bible.

As I mentioned at the start of this book, I can only tell you my story. I can't tell anyone else's story. I'm not trying to tell you how to live your life. That's not up to me. That's up to you. However, it's not normal for someone to be agnostic for the first 42 years of their life and then to choose to become a Christian because they read leadership books. I never thought I would make that choice. That is part of my transformation, so it must be a part of my story on these pages.

I didn't leave jail May 18th, 2012 planning to find God or to become a Christian. God wasn't on my radar. That is not who I was. I didn't leave jail planning to quit drinking. While reflecting on the experience during the 10 hour drive back to my home in Alabama, I made the choice to never drink alcohol again. I no longer value anything related to alcohol. I see it as a pure waste relative to *my* mission.

What I discovered while reflecting on the long drive home was hope for a better future. I had hope that if I made the right choices moving forward I could leverage the bad choices to create a better future.

During the previous four years of reading, studying, and applying leadership principles, my values had slowly begun to change. As a result, I didn't really have to give up alcohol. With clarity of purpose, vision, and hope of a better future, I no longer valued alcohol. I realized I no longer needed it in my life. It wasn't hard. It was easy.

"The ability to be successful is the ability to go from failure to failure without giving up."
~ Winston Churchill

SECTION 5

SACRIFICE IS THE FOUNDATION OF DISCIPLINE

13

SACRIFICE IS THE FOUNDATION OF DISCIPLINE

TOO OFTEN, YOU CAN'T REACH WHAT YOU NEED MOST BECAUSE YOU WON'T LET GO OF WHAT YOU WANT MOST

"Everything I've ever let go of has claw marks on it."
~ David Foster Wallace

Hope gives you a reason to make sacrifices. But, sacrificing isn't easy. It's hard. It's hard to let go of things and harder to let go of people. Yes, often to get from where you are to where you want to be, you must sacrifice relationships with people who are not helping you move forward, so you can invest your time with people who will.

Why is sacrifice so hard? Because you feel the loss immediately. And most often, the gain doesn't usually come immediately. The gain may not come for days, weeks, months, or years. Some among us make sacrifices so others may benefit. These truly special people may *never* see the gain from their sacrifice. They have paid the ultimate price for the ultimate reason: something bigger than themselves. For them, *the sacrifice was the gain.*

Unfortunately, sacrifice alone will not convert your vision into reality. When you sacrifice, you remove things from your life that are preventing you from moving forward. You rid yourself of the things and people that are tapping into your resources such as time, money, and energy. After removing the obstacles, you will be better positioned to make additional choices that will accelerate your transformation.

Recovering some of your most valuable resources is only half the battle. Once you have made additional resources available, you must intentionally use them to advance toward your preferred future (vision). You must ask and answer the following questions. Then, you must act on the answers.

- How much extra time do I have?
- How can I utilize the extra time?
- How much money have I saved?
- How can I utilize the extra money to create my preferred future?
- How can I be more effective?
- What do I need to start doing?
- What's stopping me from taking action?
- What else do I need to sacrifice?

Let's look at fitness as an example. I often hear many people who want to get fit expressing *"legitimate"* reasons as to why they can't do it. Here are some of the most common reasons I hear. *"I'm too busy." "I don't have the time." "I don't have money to join a gym."* All of those may appear to be legitimate, but they are all simply *excuses* given by people who are *unwilling to sacrifice* to get what they want.

When I hear *"I'm too busy."* or *"I don't have the time."* I often ask, *"Do you watch TV? Do you have any hobbies? Do you spend time with your friends? How long do you sleep? Do you socialize? Do you drink alcohol?"* It usually doesn't take long to figure out they are often busy doing something that's not required or that can be sacrificed if they truly want to get fit. These people don't have an issue with time. They have an issue with values. People always make time for the things they value.

When I hear *"I don't have the money to join a gym."* I ask, *"What does that have to do with getting fit?"* These people don't need a gym membership to get fit. They need to exercise. Exercise can be done in many places, *if you want to exercise.* It all comes down to one simple principle. People who want to make something happen will find a way. People who don't will find an excuse.

You must make sacrifices to get fit. You must continue to sacrifice to stay fit. And, if you want to go to a higher level of fitness or help others get fit, you will be required to sacrifice even more.

To get from where you are to where you want to be, there are two things you must do. You must develop your character and increase your competency. Those are the only two things that can and will hold you back. What do you want in life? You can have it. However, sacrifices must be made. Are you willing to pay the price? Do you have the discipline to constantly and repeatedly pay the price? Remember, thought is the foundation of choice.

As you discover and move toward your purpose, you will begin to value some things more than others. Then, those things, of lesser value, holding you back will begin to naturally drop away freeing you to intentionally move forward.

"Whenever you see a successful person, you only see the public glories, never the private sacrifices to reach them." ~ Vaibhav Shah

14

SACRIFICE DEMONSTRATES COMMITMENT

WHEN YOU GIVE UP SOMETHING OF LESSER VALUE, YOU ARE POSITIONED TO GAIN SOMETHING OF GREATER VALUE

"The price of anything is the amount of life you exchange for it." ~ Henry David Thoreau

Are you committed to reaching a higher level? Your *words will not* demonstrate your commitment. However, your *sacrifices will*. When you make sacrifices, you are communicating to the world something else is more important. Your actions convey more than a desire for a change. They convey a commitment to change.

As you work to turn your vision for your future into your reality, you will need the help and support of others. The key to gaining the support of others is based in your ability to influence them to help you move forward. When it comes to giving up something, the greater the sacrifice, the greater the influence.

However, people tend to want to keep what they have while trying to get what they want. Most likely, they have already sacrificed something to have what they have. The last thing they want to do is give it up. So, what do they do? They start spending time and energy trying to figure out how they can have both.

Far too often, when people want to get ahead, they

want someone else to make the sacrifice for them. People who aren't willing to pay the price themselves try to get others to pay the price for them. What message does this send to others? Lack of commitment. As a result, influence is diminished.

Many people want their organization to help them or the government to help them. When they can't get the help they think they deserve, they tend to blame those who won't help them. The only person to blame is in the mirror. You are ultimately responsible for your growth. If you won't invest in yourself, why should anyone else?

When you invest in the growth and development of yourself, you are communicating to others a commitment to become more valuable to others. If you choose to invest your money and time on a book, attending a developmental class, or attending a seminar, you will become more valuable, as a result of your sacrifice, to those who value what you're learning. The key is to be sure and inform those you are trying to influence: a current employer/client or a future employer/client.

If you choose to waste your time and money, you also send a message to anyone paying attention. *Your actions always reveal your values.* Wasting your money, time, and energy tells others you're okay with where you are and what you are doing. However, since you're reading this book, I'm going to assume you're not satisfied and want to make a change. If so, it's time to stop talking about changing and start changing.

First, you must demonstrate your commitment to yourself, then to others. It's time to make the sacrifice. Stop wasting your time, energy, and money on things and activities that do not increase your value. You *must* begin sacrificing and removing those things from your life.

One of the most dramatic ways to demonstrate

commitment to change is to start by changing who you associate with. That's right. Start by sacrificing personal relationships that are not moving you in the right direction. Why is this so important? Consider Jim Rohn's thoughts in this area, *"We become the combined average of the five people we hang around the most. We start to eat what they eat, drink what they drink, talk like they talk, read what they read, think like they think, watch what they watch, and dress like they dress."* We also tend to get the results they are getting.

Unfortunately for most, relationships are the hardest sacrifice to make. People often stay in bad personal relationships far too long. People also stay in bad professional relationships far too long. Both are detrimental to your preferred future. Change what needs to be changed, not what is easy to change.

Think about it. You most likely have left someone behind in order to be where you are today. They moved on, and you moved on. You changed and developed new relationships. They did too. Life went on. Don't fear change. Fear being stuck in a place you don't want to be.

You will always attract people who are like you. Most important to the attraction is your character. Therefore, if you want to attract people of higher character in your life, you must leave behind those with less character while working to improve your own. The loneliness during the transition is usually the hardest part. Many turn back. But those willing to sacrifice willingly and openly are demonstrating their commitment to a better future.

Make it happen for yourself because no one else can.

"Why do you enter into any activity with anything but commitment to achieve your objective of that activity - not a desire to achieve your objective, but a commitment?" ~ Samuel L. Parker

15

IT WAS TIME TO SACRIFICE MOST OF MY RELATIONSHIPS

OFTEN, THOSE CLOSEST TO US ARE HOLDING US BACK THE MOST

"How many of us walk around being weighed down by the baggage of our journey? You can't possibly embrace that new relationship, that new companion, that new career, that new friendship, or that new life you want while you're still holding on to the baggage of the last one. Let go...and allow yourself to embrace what is waiting for you right at your feet."
~Steve Maraboli

We choose our friends. That choice is primarily based on who we are (our character) and who they are (their character). We choose to be around people with character similar to ours, and they do the exact same. If either person detects too much variation, the relationship won't last or will be distant at best.

By the time I got home from Texas, I had already realized my life was about to radically change. It was time to sacrifice all of the personal relationships I had made with others like me: those who enjoyed wasting their time drinking alcohol like I had done for nearly 30 years.

I wouldn't be hanging out with them any longer. I wouldn't be inviting them over to the pool in the summer or to the hot tub in the winter. I wouldn't be accepting invitations to hang out with them because I knew what they would be doing: wasting time drinking alcohol.

Deciding to stop drinking was easy. Deciding to distance myself from most of my friends wasn't so easy. I did it. But, it wasn't easy. I didn't think I was better than any of them. I still don't believe I'm better than any of them. What I began to think is that I was simply different.

Because I had been reading, applying, and teaching leadership content for the last four years, I was beginning to think much different than my friends who were happily coasting along without any intentional growth in their lives. Since I was becoming different than most of them, we were also beginning to move in different directions. It was simply time to make a drastic change.

When we have a desire to grow to a higher level of effectiveness and a desire to be around exceptional people operating at a higher level than we currently are, we must leave those people in our lives who are like us behind and choose to become exceptional ourselves. This is the only way we will attract and retain relationships with higher level, exceptional people.

You cannot attract and sustain a relationship with someone at a higher level of awareness for very long unless you are truly operating at their level. If you are trying to hang on to the lower level relationships of the past, it sends a signal to those who are operating at a higher level. They will recognize you aren't truly there yet.

Exceptional people have a higher level of awareness. Can you attract them temporarily? Sure. Can you maintain the relationship long term? It's not going to happen. They will see right through you.

Knowing we become the average of the five people we hang around the most, choosing our friends will play a significant role in our ability to grow and develop. Unless our friends have a desire to grow and develop with us, they cannot help us. They will only hinder us.

Letting go is common sense, but it's not common practice. Why? Letting go of friends is not easy. It's hard.

There is a trick to pulling this off. You can't be with one type/group of people one day and start associating with a different type/group of people the next day. It doesn't work like that. It takes time.

Here is the three step process most aren't willing to go through:

1) You must choose to leave behind people who are currently attracted to who you are today. You haven't changed yet, you simply have a desire to change.

2) While suspended between those you were associated with and those you want to be associated with, you must go it alone while developing and growing yourself into the type person you want to attract. You must be strong and intentional.

3) You must wait patiently to attract people with higher level character. You have left behind people who want you back. You haven't yet built new higher level relationships because you won't meet those you're seeking until you are operating consistently at their level.

You must resist going back. If you do go back, you must start over. You must continue doing the necessary work at Step 2 until you attract the kind of people you want to be associated with at Step 3. If you can't attract them, you haven't done enough work or haven't done it long enough. It's not their fault. It's your fault.

"If you want a better life personally and/or professionally, you have to ask yourself this question, 'Who am I surrounding myself with, day to day?' Those who support and create energy for change? Or those who are stuck in the comfort of what is?"
~ Henry Cloud

SECTION 6

DISCIPLINE IS THE FOUNDATION OF GROWTH

16

DISCIPLINE IS THE FOUNDATION OF GROWTH

YOU MUST TO DO THE RIGHT THING AT THE RIGHT TIME FOR THE RIGHT REASON

"When it comes to self-discipline, people choose one of two things: Either they choose the pain of discipline, which comes from sacrifice and growth, or they choose the pain of regret, which comes from taking the easy road and missing opportunities."
~ John C. Maxwell

You must develop discipline. Discipline is the catalyst for growth. The more discipline you have, the more growth you will achieve. As you progress from knowing what to do and begin doing what should be done, you are crossing the bridge called discipline. Discipline allows you to turn your dreams, goals, and vision into reality.

Discipline is giving yourself a command and following through with it. You must do the right thing for the right reasons at the right time in order to be effective.

When you take the right steps toward your vision, discipline will allow you to convert your sacrifice into growth. Growth is about reaching and stretching. John Maxwell often speaks about the *"Law of the Rubber Band"* saying, *"People are like rubber bands, we are only adding value when we are being stretched."* Discipline causes you to stretch yourself.

It takes very little effort to stand out in today's society.

Many people in school, college, and the military cannot wait to get finished, get a job, move away from intentional focused learning, and get comfortable.

With discipline, those continuing to educate themselves intentionally by developing their specialized knowledge steadily and consistently increase their potential to do more, earn more, and be more. Consider these impactful words from Napoleon Hill, *"Successful people, in all callings, never stop acquiring specialized knowledge related to their major purpose, business, or profession. Those who are not successful usually make the mistake of believing that the 'knowledge-acquiring' period ends when one finishes school. The truth is that formal education does but little more than to put one in the way of learning how to acquire practical knowledge."*

With discipline, it is not hard to separate yourself from the crowd. Many people don't attempt to develop and reach their full potential. They simply get comfortable with no desire to grow and stretch themselves any farther. I've read various surveys stating 30-40% of high school and college students never read another book after graduation. Why? They lack discipline.

You can easily become exceptional. But, it won't just happen. You must become intentional about developing the discipline that will allow you to make it happen on purpose in pursuit of your vision.

The key is to get into the minds of those already where you want to be. Those already doing what you want to do. You can read books. You may know someone willing to mentor you in person or by phone. As long as you are constantly growing your mind in the area of character, your passion and purpose, you cannot go wrong.

Humble people understand the more they learn, the more they realize what they have yet to learn. They know they will never learn it all. They see the opportunities for growth ahead. They become disciplined lifetime learners and continue to run the race knowing there truly is no finish line. Having a title, a position, or a degree doesn't mean they have crossed the finish line.

Those who are humble are like sponges soaking up knowledge because they are eager for growth. Our character determines how we learn, what we learn, and how much we learn. Discipline turns desire into growth.

As you move forward, don't focus on earning more. Focus on *learning* more. Increasing your value is a simple concept. It's always easy to understand, but it's not always easy to do. Discipline is the key.

Your value to others will increase as you read, learn, grow, and apply. It's a never ending process. Do not set a fixed goal and stop after reaching it. You must understand growth is infinite. You want to be growth-oriented, not goal-oriented. Therefore, make *continuous growth* your main goal. Use small, short term goals to support the main goal.

The most important person you will ever influence is yourself. The degree to which you're able to influence yourself will determine the level of influence you ultimately have with others. Typically, when we are talking about leading ourselves, the word most commonly used to describe self-leadership is discipline. You must practice discipline daily to maintain your personal integrity and to increase your influence with others. Discipline is not something you practice only when you feel like it. Discipline is something you practice daily because it's necessary.

"The pain of discipline weighs ounces.
Regret weighs tons." ~ Jim Rohn

17

DISCIPLINE LEVERAGES SACRIFICE

THE GREATER THE DISCIPLINE,
THE GREATER THE REWARD

"Nothing can stop the man with the right mental attitude from achieving his goals; nothing on earth can help the man with the wrong mental attitude."
~ Thomas Jefferson

The key to moving beyond average is doing what exceptional people do, not wanting what they have. When you see others doing what you want to be doing, the question you must answer is not, *"Do I want to be doing what they are doing?"* But rather, *"Do I want to do what they had to do to get to do what they are doing?"*

Your answer to the first question communicates you have an interest in doing it. Your answer to the second question communicates whether you will have a chance to do it. Deciding to do something and paying the price to actually get to do it are two very different things. Deciding to do something doesn't require sacrifice. However, paying the price to do something will require sacrifice.

Remember, sacrifice is giving up something. The amount of discipline you develop will determine the value you are able to leverage from the sacrifice.

For example, if you enroll in a college class or to attend some type of development seminar, the sacrifice will be the money and the time. Because you are sacrificing your money to grow and develop yourself, you will not be able to use it for anything else. It will be gone. It won't be available for dining out or to put toward a weekend getaway. And, the time you invest in attending the required class cannot be used to do anything else.

The sacrifice only creates an opportunity for growth. It does not create the growth. Only discipline will create growth and allow you to make the additional sacrifices of time necessary to study, learn, and apply what you're learning. Discipline leverages sacrifice. It's a two part formula: SACRIFICE + DISCIPLINE = GROWTH.

The growth cycle must be repeated constantly. Sacrifice something. Demonstrate discipline. Achieve growth. Sacrifice something. Demonstrate discipline. Achieve growth. Sacrifice something. Demonstrate discipline. Achieve growth.

If you have the discipline to repeat the growth cycle, you can become exceptional in your area of interest (passion/purpose) quickly. Why? Because most people will only do what they have to do, which is not much.

Most people can become an expert in their area of passion and purpose in a few years by simply reading books, magazines, and articles followed by application of what they are learning. Most won't have to attend college or receive any formal education. They must only apply themselves by choosing to invest their time instead of wasting their time.

Obviously, if you want to enter a profession that requires a formal education such as practicing law or medicine, you must earn a college degree. However, the growth cycle must still be consistently applied. The cycle is a principle for growth. It applies in all situations.

If you don't repeat the growth cycle, you will become stagnant and begin to slip backward. As the world changes at ever increasing speeds, there is no option to remain still. You are either growing or slowing, moving forward or backward. Everything around you is constantly changing. You must also be constantly changing. If not, you may think you're holding steady, but you're not. At some point, you will pay the price for not having the discipline to continue growing and developing yourself as you get passed by those who do.

Another way to leverage sacrifice using discipline is to execute efficiently and effectively. In other words, you must have the discipline to develop an effective plan that allows you to address the most important things you need to learn and do on the front end. You must be methodical and intentional to leverage discipline.

Take the time and do the work necessary to determine what the most important thing that must be done is. Brainstorm a list of all the things you're aware of that must be done to move you from where you are to where you want to be. Then, ask yourself, *"What's the most important thing that I must do?"* Identify the one thing that if you don't do it, the other things won't matter? Now, do it. If you haven't invested in personal growth and development, that's usually the first place to start.

Too often, people without discipline focus on doing the easy things first. Why? Because it's easy. They jump from one easy thing to the next. Unfortunately, most people who attempt to leverage their sacrifice this way end up wasting their sacrifice. They simply don't have the discipline to do the hard work of doing what's most important first: personal character development.

Don't accept your circumstances. Design them.

*"We are not victims of our situation.
We are the architects of it."* ~ Simon Sinek

18

DEVELOPING THE DISCIPLINE TO INVEST IN MYSELF

IT WAS TIME TO START LIVING MY LIFE BY DESIGN INSTEAD OF BY DEFAULT

"There are 24 hours in a day. What will you do with yours? If you write, you will become an author. If you exercise, you will become an athlete. If you study, you will become an expert. Your life is a result of how you invest your time." ~ Denard Ash

As I share my personal stories, don't get too caught up in the story. It's my story, not yours. *Focus on the principles* found in my story and learn how to apply them in your life.

Giving up alcohol, the fun I had hanging out wasting my time, and those friends who continued to value it was how I applied the principle of sacrifice. That may not be what you need to sacrifice. You may have other issues. You may watch a lot of TV, play a lot of games on your TV or your favorite electronic device, you may waste hours on social media, you may be a very reactive or negative person, you may have poor eating habits, or have a tobacco problem, or one of thousands of others things that may be holding you back.

I never had a daily drinking problem. I was the social drinker. I would go weeks or sometimes months without drinking at all. But, I was always looking for an opportunity to hang out with friends and have a few drinks (usually too many). I looked forward to tailgating at football games and holiday weekends. What I was really sacrificing when I gave up alcohol, and the friends that valued what I had valued, was all the fun I used to have and the many ways I had it.

There usually isn't one thing holding us back. There are usually many small things and a few big things that together have a negative impact on our lives.

Giving up fun things is hard! But, as I continued down my transformational path, I found more meaningful ways to have fun. I simply had to stay the course and trust the process.

What we all have in common is this: we all have room for character improvement. Our character is what is holding us all back. You must figure out your way forward. I must figure out my way forward. The key is learning how to apply the principles I'm sharing throughout this book to create a better future for yourself. I simply share my stories as an example to help you see how I have applied them to get positive results.

After more than 20 years in the blue-collar manufacturing world, I thought that was where I would spend all of my working years. After giving up drinking alcohol and sacrificing the relationships with those who continued to value drinking, partying, and consistently wasting their time and mine, it was time to leverage my newly reclaimed resources: my time and my money.

Instead of wasting money on a trip to the beach, a trip to the mountains, or a cruise, all of which would include wasting my time and money drinking alcohol, I began to invest much more time and money to intentionally develop myself. From 2008-2012, I had only been purchasing books and reading consistently to become more effective in my consulting business. It wasn't truly about developing my character. It was about getting better results at work, and I did.

My favorite quote from Les Brown is, *"Coincidence is God's way of staying anonymous." Coincidentally* in June 2012 while I was still agnostic and less than a month after I had decided to transform myself, I was sitting at my computer looking up something on the internet and discovered John Maxwell was offering a one day seminar on book writing that month. He is the top leadership guru in the world and has published nearly 100 books on leadership. After four years of reading leadership books, I was anxious to write my own. In my mind, John was the best to learn from, plus I liked his character and his style.

The cost was substantial considering I had never invested more than $20 or $30 for a book. I also wanted to intentionally invest in my son, Eric. I registered us both. The cost was well over $1,000 to attend the event and to travel to West Palm Beach, Florida for several days. Wasting a $1,000 to have fun had been common in the past. Investing $1,000 to grow myself was new.

While at the event, I learned about a 3-day leadership certification John was offering in August 2012. I didn't hesitate to register us both. The investment for us to attend would be over $12,000! I didn't think twice about it. I was beginning to live life on purpose.

We get out of life what we are willing to invest into it...plain and simple. Invest a lot, get a lot. Invest a little, get a little. What will it be? What needs to change? What are you willing to change? What are you willing to invest?

"If you have too little confidence, you will think you can't learn. If you have too much, you will think you don't have to learn." ~ Eric Hoffer

SECTION 7

GROWTH IS THE FOUNDATION OF CHANGE

19

GROWTH IS THE FOUNDATION OF CHANGE

IF YOU'RE NOT GROWING, YOU'RE SLOWING

"When I go through change it is because I am passive; I accept it as inevitable. So, I sigh and say, I hope this comes out all right. When I grow through change, I become active. I take control of my attitude, my emotions. Years ago, I determined that while others may lead small lives, I would not; while others may become victims, I would not; and while others will leave their future in other's hands, I will not. And while others go through life, I will grow through it. That is my choice, and I will surrender it to no one."
~ John C. Maxwell

You can change without growing. However, you can't grow without changing. You can create change or be impacted by change caused by others. Change may, and often does, just happen. Most change is outside of your control.

Growth is much different. Growth doesn't just happen. It doesn't simply come with age. If it did, all of the older people would be more successful than all of the younger people. That's simply not how it works. You must make a choice to be intentional about your growth.

As you continue learning about *The 10 Foundational Elements of Intentional Transformation*, understand all the foundational layers you've learned so far support your growth. The foundational layer of growth that's just been added will support the following foundational layers: change, success, and significance. Each layer is supported by those that come before it. And, each layer helps support all of those that come after it.

This book was written in a methodical and sequential way to support you in any area where you desire change and transformation. It's sequentially assembled to allow you to better understand how the various layers support and are supported by each other. The principles you're learning can be applied to any area of your life, personally and professionally.

Let's refer back to the previous example of fitness. You will not become fit accidentally. No one else can make you fit. You must do it. Likewise, you will not grow accidentally. No one else can grow you. You will always be responsible for growing yourself. These thoughts bring to mind a quote from an unknown source, *"You can lead a human to knowledge, but you can't make them think."*

You must develop an intentional growth plan that will move you toward your vision. As you move along the path of transformation, you will be able to see more and see farther. As you expand your vison, you must also make adjustments to your growth plan to remain highly effective and efficient. Intentional growth based on your passion will always lead you closer to discovering your *why*, your purpose.

Remember, you will be much more effective if you are primarily growth-oriented and secondarily goal-oriented. That does not mean you do not set goals. You should always set goals that support your *continuous* growth. Keep in mind, the goal of growth is not change for the sake of change. Change can be positive or negative. Negative change will not serve you well.

The goal of growth is positive change. What determines if change is positive? Positive change moves you closer to realizing your vision, creating your preferred future, and allows you to live a life more closely aligned with your purpose.

Where will you see the most benefit relative to your growth? Character growth will always produce the greatest results because it acts as a multiplier relative to your competency. Relative to character, you will see the most positive change when you work in your areas of *weakness*. When it comes to growing and developing your character, focus on developing your integrity, not creating your image.

The second area where your growth will show up is in your competency. However, when working to create positive change relative to your competency, you should always work in your areas of *strength* where you are naturally gifted. Character will take you most of the way, and competency will take you the rest of the way.

It's worth mentioning again. As you grow, you will likely need to leave some people behind. They may not be going where you're going. You may be able to influence them to grow with you. If not, you should not allow them to hold you back. They make their choices. You make your choices. You can still love them while you're missing them. Your journey through life is not their journey through life. We're all on a different mission.

To live more abundantly, you must move forward.

"Where there is no belief or hope for growth to be real, it is no longer attempted. People, or organizations, enter into a state of sameness, and as we have seen, that is really when things are no longer alive. Death is taking over not growth." ~ Henry Cloud

20

GROWTH CREATES OPTIONS

WHEN YOU GROW YOURSELF, YOU ATTRACT NEW OPPORTUNITIES

"The moment you take responsibility for everything in your life is the moment you can change anything in your life." ~ Hal Elrod

Growth will *always* increase your influence. When you increase your influence, you *will* increase your options.

Instead of taking the risk of investing in themselves along the way, too many people play it safe and invest in their retirement. They value having money and comfort later instead of growth and options now. The result: many people live an unfulfilled, safe, *and often miserable*, life dreaming about the opportunity to escape from it all, to retire, to truly quit living and start waiting. *Waiting to die.*

That is not a life. That is an existence. What's stopping you from living a better and more fulfilling life today?

Most people seek *security* and *stability* in their lives. However, what they need in order to truly excel, become the best version of themselves, and create their preferred future is *freedom* and *options*.

You must continuously follow your passion to find your purpose. If you don't like what you're doing, why are you doing it? There's only one reason, you don't have options? Why? You're not focused on growing. You're focused on coasting. I read the following on a sign outside a church many years ago, *"If the truth hurts, it probably should."*

Too many of us think we're on a journey, but we're not. We may have started out strong, but as we went farther down the path and things got harder, we took a seat on the first bench we saw and have been there ever since watching others pass us by. If you're on the bench, it's time for you to get up, get going again, and make a bigger difference in the world.

Don't know where to start? Start with your world, the one best seen when looking in a mirror. Start with you.

Most of your options will not be created between 9am and 5pm. While you're busy working, someone else is in control. Someone else is determining your agenda. They are paying you to do what they want done. There's not a lot of time for intentional growth and development.

If you're serious about creating options for yourself, you must create them between 5pm and 9am. You decide what you do when you're not at work. What you do when you're not at work determines when you work, how much you work, what work you do, and how much you get paid to work. This is where sacrifice and discipline are key to your growth. How you spend or invest your time away from work is up to you. What needs to change?

When it comes to increasing your options, you can work in the area of character or competency. Several research studies have revealed **87% of our results/influence come from our character** and only 13% of our results/influence come from our competency.

Before you get to do what it is you want to do, you must influence someone to give you a chance. The key to getting the chance will first be based on your character. However, it often takes time to learn someone's true character. Therefore, some people with character issues are given a chance they don't deserve. In this case, it is later taken away. People are usually hired for what they know (competency), but often they are later fired for who they are (character).

As you become intentional about growth, I suggest investing 80% of your time and resources on character development. Your character growth will allow you to attract others with higher level character. Others who can help you. Others who have greater influence than those with less character. The more you develop your character, the better your social network will become.

Intentionally invest the other 20% of your time and resources on competency development. Focus on the areas you're naturally interested in and gifted in. No one can compete with someone who has a passion and a fire burning inside them. Don't flow with the current. Choose your destination.

You may not be doing what you want to do now. That's okay. Start where you are and grow your way to where you want to be. As you work on your character and develop your competency in your area of interest, you will naturally start to attract others with the same interest. As you do, you will be presented with new opportunities and options. The opportunities are there waiting for you now.

Then, if you're willing to continue sacrificing and growing, you will begin to reshape your career and be well on your way to creating your preferred future.

"On the path to your God-inspired future, attractive alternatives will be offered. You will be presented with more money, a better position, or a more sedate lifestyle in a more comfortable geographic location. You are going to face other kinds of more dramatic temptations as well. We all do. But, we have to constantly remember our future." ~ Terry A. Smith

21

THE IMPACT OF INTENTIONAL GROWTH

WHEN I BEGAN TO LIVE ON PURPOSE, I DISCOVERED MY PURPOSE

"You must have a long-range vision to keep you from being frustrated by short-range failures."
~ Charles Noble

After attending the *"A Day About Books"* event with John Maxwell in June 2012 and registering for the leadership certification in August 2012, Eric and I could hardly wait for the next two months to pass. It's amazing how much can change in a few months when we become intentional about living our lives on purpose.

A few months earlier I had been coasting through life with no worries in the world. That was before I made the choice that initiated my transformation. If you would have asked me how things were before that night in May, I would have told you I was loving life because I was.

I had done very well considering I had started my life on the front lines as a machine operator in the blue-collar manufacturing industry. My consulting business had produced great financial results, and Ria had worked her way into a Director's position at the hospital. Ria and I were earning well into the six figures annually by 2012.

We had a nice home, nice cars, expensive mountain bikes, other toys, and pretty much whatever we wanted.

In the eyes of most, we were very successful. What I wanted most was to have as much fun as I could. We were always traveling somewhere having fun and enjoying life.

I thought that was what life was about. I thought I was supposed to work hard, so I could have the things I wanted. Once I had the things I wanted, I thought the rest of our money was for having fun and enjoying life. At least, that's what I had witnessed most people doing my entire life. They were either making a lot of money and having a lot of fun. Or, they were trying to make a lot of money, so they could have a lot of fun.

By August 2012, I was beginning to realize I could use the extra money for something other than fun. Instead of wasting it, we could begin investing it. What is better to invest your hard earned money in than yourself? What was interesting was how easy it had been for me to waste money and how hard it was to invest money in myself.

When we waste it, we get the *"quick fix"* from the fun or enjoyment we get from whatever it is we wasted it on. However, when we invest it in our own growth and development, we then must go to work applying what we've learned as we try to achieve results at a higher level. The reward usually doesn't come instantly. It typically comes many months later, and sometimes, many years later.

The three days at the John Maxwell event in August 2012 raised my level of awareness. It was exactly what I needed. It helped me realize my true potential. I began to believe I could make a bigger difference with more people at a higher level. There were hundreds of people from all around the world at the event. They were there intentionally invest in and grow themselves too.

After talking with many of them, I began to realize

when it came to understanding leadership, I was already far ahead of most. At the time, I had already led leaders and their cross-functional teams through over 11,000 hours of process improvement, organizational change, and cultural transformation. I had been learning and applying it very intentionally in my professional life.

My choices in May 2012 had served as a catalyst only because I had grown so much the previous four years. The timing was right. It was another *coincidence*.

Everything John Maxwell spoke about at the event resonated with me at a new level. I was ready to hear it. I already knew I wanted to write leadership books. But after those three days, I knew I also wanted to do what John was doing. I wanted to be on a stage motivating and inspiring people all over the world to improve their lives and the lives of others.

During the event, we learned about a higher level mentorship program John was offering. Once again, I didn't hesitate to invest in the program for me and Eric. This required another $6,000 investment. I had invested nearly $20,000 in the two of us in just a few months. This led to Ria and my mom also being certified. Today, we have invested well over $100,000 in our growth and development over the last four years. It wasn't wasted.

My growth revealed my purpose: I wanted a career in professional leadership development. Because I was expanding, my vision for a better future was expanding.

"Into the hands of every individual is given a marvelous power for good or evil - the silent, unconscious, unseen influence of his life. This is simply the constant radiation of what man really is, not what he pretends to be." ~ William George Jordan

SECTION 8

CHANGE IS THE FOUNDATION OF SUCCESS

22

CHANGE IS THE FOUNDATION OF SUCCESS

IF YOU ALREADY KNEW WHAT YOU NEED TO KNOW, YOU WOULD ALREADY BE WHERE YOU WANT TO GO

"Those who cannot change their minds cannot change anything." ~ George Bernard Shaw

Without change, there can be no improvement. But, as you've already learned, the change you seek should be positive. Negative change will not bring about success. The change being discussed on these pages is the change created by your intentional growth. Positive change created by you.

Changing doesn't mean you will become more successful. You must change the right things for the right reasons. If you truly want success, don't focus on changing to become successful. Focus first on changing to become more valuable. As you become more valuable, you *will* become more successful. The most valuable people are also the most successful people.

Creating positive change takes courage. I remember the words of Anais Nin, *"Life shrinks or expands in proportion to one's courage."* Positive change begins as thoughts in the mind. But, it's courage that will allow you to convert those thoughts into positive change.

The remainder of this chapter is an excerpt from,

Change Happens: Leading Yourself and Others through Change, a book I co-authored with my wife, Ria.

Change has the power to launch you into a new career, a new relationship, a new city, and even a new way of thinking. When you change what you do, you change what you get. Saying *no* to the *wrong* things frees you up to say *yes* to the *right* things. What you say yes to *shapes* your future. Saying no to something old gives you the *freedom* to say yes to something new.

Without the courage to change, you will get left behind by those brave enough to take risks and fail their way to a better future. Failure isn't really the appropriate word to use. Failure is actually often misused. People use the word failure as an excuse not to try something. However, it's only failure if you quit and never try again.

As a baby, you fell endless times as you attempted to walk. Try. Fail. Try. Fail. Try. Fail. But, that's not really what happened. In the end, did you fail to walk, or did you learn to walk? You learned to walk like the rest of us.

What really happened was this. Try. Learn. Try. Learn. Try. Learn. Try. Succeed. Find something new to learn. Repeat.

The rest of life should be the same way. It took courage then, and it'll take more courage to try new things now. Why? Because when you were learning to walk, you received endless encouragement from everyone around you. And most often, when you would fall, someone would pick you up. Learning as an adult is a bit harder.

Things are different once you grow up. As an adult, you will mostly receive a lot of doubting questions and negative feedback from other adults. If babies could talk and understand each other, they would probably never learn to walk. Could you imagine what it would be like in the nursery listening to the babies talking?

- Why do you want to walk?
- Don't you think you might fall?
- I tried that once, and it didn't work.
- Have you considered what will happen if you do fall?
  I bet it will really hurt!
- I saw Danny try that last week. He fell, broke his
  nose, and cried for hours.
- Have you thought about what will happen once you
  get going? How will you stop?

I was having a little fun with you, but I'm sure you get the point. That's what adults do all day long. You've heard those voices. They try to talk other adults out of trying something new because they're afraid themselves. If you want to get to a new level, you've got to change how you invest your time and who you invest it with.

You need to be reading, watching videos, or listening to audios of people who are doing what you want to be doing or that have done what you want to do. Whatever you do, don't seek advice about your life and your future from anyone who has not been where you want to go.

They don't know how to get there, and they don't want to go. Why would you ever give them a right to veto your dream? You shouldn't. Don't do it!

> *"The first step toward success is taken when you refuse to be a captive of the environment you first find yourself in." ~ Mark Caine*

23

CHANGE RELEASES POTENTIAL

WITHOUT CHANGE, YOUR POTENTIAL CAN NEVER BECOME YOUR REALITY

"When we are faced with change, we either step forward into growth, or we step backward into safety." ~ Abraham Maslow

Are you playing small? What are you leaving on the table? Your potential is your reality. You can verify this because where you are now is not where you used to be? Why? You have already realized some of your potential, your untapped reality. Therefore, your potential today can also become your reality tomorrow.

Georg Lichtenburg made the following observation, *"I cannot say whether things will get better if we change; what I can say is they must change if they are to get better."* When everything is constantly changing, the challenge is also changing. What was mastered successfully yesterday may no longer be relevant today. Therefore, the one thing that should also constantly change is *you* and *me*. If we're not willing to change, we should expect to be left behind by those who are.

When we choose to constantly change to meet new challenges, we have a chance to continue to achieve personal and organizational success. But, when we refuse to change in response to new and greater challenges, we and the organizations where we work will struggle to survive, and some will end up taking a dive.

Just as you were able to leverage sacrifice for your benefit, you can also leverage change for your benefit. Leverage (the verb) is defined as *"using a quality or advantage to obtain a desired result."*

As Ria Story wrote in *Change Happens*, *"When we leverage something, we take advantage of the lever to multiply the results of our efforts. Leveraging something can be a powerful way to gain momentum and accelerate progress. But, we seldom think of change as something we can, or should, leverage."* If you're not leveraging change, you're missing a great opportunity to accelerate your journey to a higher level of success.

Ria continues, *"Change always brings opportunities. When we leverage change we not only take advantage of the obvious opportunities, we create new ones as well. In order to leverage change and take advantage of or create opportunities, we first must see them. Then, we must be willing to put forth the effort to maximize them."*

When it comes to change, who will potentially receive the most benefit? Someone who resists change or someone who embraces change? No doubt, the person embracing change will be more likely to turn their potential into success. Once you've made the choice to embrace change, don't stop there.

As you begin leveraging change, there will be many benefits that will help you achieve greater success. Leverage the change for maximum benefit. Leveraging change means doing more than simply making the change. Leveraging change means you will seek ways to intentionally grow your influence during the change.

Those who are neutral or resistant to change will never receive the benefits associated with leveraging change. As you already know, most people don't like change and put their energy into resisting and complaining. When others are moaning, groaning, and whining, it's easy for you to start shining.

As Denis Waitley remarked, *"A sign of wisdom and maturity is when you come to terms with the realization that your decisions cause your rewards and consequences. You are responsible for your life, and your ultimate success depends on the choices you make."* When you choose to be proactive while everyone else is being reactive, that mindset is already allowing you to leverage change to your benefit. By changing the way you think, you're able to turn your potential into success.

High impact leaders intentionally embrace, leverage, and initiate change. They are also aware of others who do the same. You can unleash your potential when you focus on increasing your influence with game changers. They operate at an entirely different level and tend to operate with others who exhibit the same level of character when it comes to change.

When it comes to leveraging change there's a magic word you can proactively use to begin separating yourself from the crowd in a way that allows you to get *noticed* by the high impact leaders and *promoted* for the right reasons. The magic word is *"HOW."*

When you ask, *"How can I?"* or *"How can we?"* instead of *"Can I?"* or *"Can we?"* you have started to truly transform the way you and others think. *"Can I?"* indicates self-doubt. You don't know if you can. But, when you say *"How can I?"* you have already decided you will and you can. Therefore, your imagination can run wild in the right direction. *"How can I?"* lets you know there is a way. You just need to discover it.

"Small, Smart Choices + Consistency + Time = RADICAL DIFFERENCE" ~ Darren Hardy

24

A CHANGE I DIDN'T SEE COMING

WHEN WE EXPERIENCE THE RIGHT CHANGE, THE RIGHT THINGS CHANGE

"Without change, something sleeps inside us, and seldom awakens. The sleeper must awaken."
~ Frank Herbert

Three months after a bad choice landed me in jail for a night, I was still following through on the commitment I had made to myself. I was continuing to transform. I wasn't only saying it. I was doing it.

I had already done something I had never done before. I had invested thousands of dollars in my personal character development. I had invested many hours into taking my character development to the next level. I had literally left behind an old way of thinking and living.

At the three day certification with John Maxwell in August 2012, John held a church service on the last morning of the training. John had spent the first 25 years of his career as a pastor. Since there were hundreds of people from all around the world, there were many different religions represented at the event. John told us in advance he would be leading a volunteer service early on the last day. He said, *"Feel free to come, but don't feel obligated to come."*

Being agnostic all of my life and having no opinion about God one way or the other, attending a church service wasn't something I did very often. Usually, it would be when Ria asked me to go to her grandparent's church for some special occasion. I hated it, but I went because I knew it mattered to her and to them.

I was always very uncomfortable as a non-believer in a room surrounded by believers. I didn't have a clue what they were talking about. I didn't have a clue about the customs. I didn't have a clue about the songs they were singing. I didn't want to sing. I would stand there while everyone else was singing. I wasn't comfortable until I was back in the car leaving the church.

By August 2012, I had come to realize over the last four years of reading and studying leadership, especially when I started reading John's content, that I was aligning myself with Christian principles. I was okay with that because I believed in them. I wasn't threatened by them. Believing in a principle didn't mean I believed in God. I was safe. I could use the principles to get better results.

Throughout my life, I had discovered two things about Christians:

    1. Not all Christians are good people.

    2. Most really good people are Christians.

I wasn't attracted to many Christians because they were telling the world they were Christians and living like they weren't.

For me, that represents a huge character flaw and a major integrity problem. I wasn't claiming to be a Christian, and I wasn't living like one in some areas of my life. At least, my actions were in alignment with my words. Many Christians are very much out of alignment.

This is one reason I still don't want to be involved with a church or the masses of people that attend a church. I don't hang around people that say one thing and do another. It doesn't matter if they are Christians, atheists, or something else. I intentionally associate with people of high character who live with integrity.

I chose to attend John's service the last day. My decision had nothing to do with the spiritual aspect of the service. I simply liked hearing John speak about anything. This was an extra opportunity to do that. The service was great. John taught about religion in a way that resonated with me. He spoke the same way about religion as he did about leadership. The only difference was the references to scripture. I actually enjoyed it.

But, he did something at the end of the service I wasn't expecting. During the last prayer, he asked everyone to keep their heads down except those who didn't have a relationship with Christ. He asked those like me to look at him because he wanted to talk directly to us. I wanted to pretend I was a believer, but my personal integrity caused me to raise my head and admit I wasn't.

After he spoke a powerful and personal message to us, he said, *"Raise your hand and keep it up if you want to accept Christ today."* For whatever reason, unexpectedly, I raised my hand, repeated after him, and accepted Christ into my life. I would have never imagined that was going to happen when I walked into the room that morning. I was simply going to hear John speak.

I'm reminded of the Darren Hardy quote I shared at the end of the last chapter, *"Small, smart choices + consistency + time = RADICAL DIFFERENCE."* Four years of small, smart choices consistently allowed me to effectively leverage a bad choice. Accepting Christ was my biggest signal to the world I was truly transforming myself.

"Things do not change; we change."
~ Henry David Thoreau

SECTION 9

SUCCESS IS THE FOUNDATION OF SIGNIFICANCE

25

SUCCESS IS THE FOUNDATION OF SIGNIFICANCE

TO BE SUCCESSFUL, YOU MUST FOCUS ON BECOMING MORE VALUABLE, NOT MORE SUCCESSFUL

"Your ability to achieve your own happiness is the true measure of your success in life. Nothing is more important. Nothing can replace it. If you accomplish everything of a material nature, but you are not happy, you have actually 'failed' at fulfilling your potential as a human being." ~ Brian Tracy

The most successful people are those who help others become successful. However, until you create a high level of success for yourself, it's not likely that you will be in a position to help others become highly successful. The remainder of this book is intended to help you understand what it truly means to be successful, significant, and ultimately, to leave a legacy.

If you choose to develop the habits of success, you'll make success a habit. Successful people have the habit of intentionally investing time and money into growing themselves because they value themselves and know this truth: Life IS hard! So, they take responsibility to make life a little easier by developing themselves. As a result, they are able to *achieve better results.*

When it comes to creating success, the words of Norman Vincent Peale ring true, *"Believe in yourself! Have faith in your abilities! Without a humble but reasonable confidence in your powers, you cannot be successful or happy."* This is why the habit of intentionally growing and developing yourself is key. Your growth in your area of passion and purpose will give you confidence. You will quickly separate yourself from those who are coasting through life.

No matter how much someone else believes in you, you must ultimately believe in yourself. You can borrow belief from others to get going, but to be highly effective, you must believe in yourself. You can generate this belief and confidence from within by simply leading yourself well in the direction you want to go.

The byproduct of growth and development is belief and confidence. The byproduct of belief and confidence is success. Consider the wisdom in the words of St. Francis of Assisi, *"Start doing what is necessary; then, do what is possible; and suddenly you are doing the impossible."* To be successful, you must start where you are and do what you can. Do this consistently and endlessly, and you will become highly successful. Discipline is the key to success.

Do you dream about a higher level of success?

This question reminds me of a story about an old Army general sitting at the bar of an officer's club staring at his third martini. A brand-new second lieutenant comes in and spots him. He can't resist sitting next to the general and starting up a conversation. The old general patiently listens to the kid and courteously answers his questions. After a time, the second lieutenant gets to what he really wants to know. *"How do you make general?"* he asks with raw, unconcealed ambition.

"Well son," said the old general, *"here's what you do. You work like a dog, you never stop studying, you train your troops hard, and you take care of them. You are loyal to your commander and your soldiers. You do the best you can in every mission, and you*

love the Army. You are ready to die for the mission and your troops. That's all you have to do."

The second lieutenant replied with a soft, young voice, *"Wow, and that's how you make general?"*

"Naw!" bellowed the old general. *"That's how you make first lieutenant. Just keep doing all of the things I told you and let 'em see what you've got,"* said the general, finishing off his last martini as he turned to walk away.

The old general was saying to the young second lieutenant that in order to be successful he would need to make a career out of serving others. The general told him to start with development of himself. Then, grow and develop others. Then, serve everyone and be willing to sacrifice for the mission and your team if necessary. That's what serving looks like through the eyes of an old general. He basically gave a class about success and significance with a few short sentences.

Success looks different for everyone. Don't measure yourself against others who appear successful. For you to be successful, you simply must be better tomorrow than you are today as you strive to turn your vision for a preferred future into reality. That is success. When you're able to move from where you are and get closer to where you want to be, you're traveling down the road to success.

Success will always create momentum, and momentum will always create the opportunity for more success.

"When a challenge in life is met by a response that is equal to it, you have success. But when the challenge moves to a higher level, the old, once successful response no longer works - it fails; thus, nothing fails like success." ~ Stephen R. Covey

26

SUCCESS CREATES MOMENTUM

WHEN YOU CREATE MOMENTUM, DON'T REST UPON IT. BUILD UPON IT.

"Where success is concerned, people are not measured in inches, or pounds, or college degrees, or family background; they are measured by the size of their thinking. How big we think determines the size of our accomplishments." ~ David Schwartz

When it comes to achieving success, momentum is your best friend. As with sacrifice and change, momentum can also be leveraged. When you're able to generate momentum, don't miss the opportunity to leverage it for additional success. Your goal should always be to *maximize momentum.*

Far too often, when someone creates momentum, the first thing they tend to do is take it easy and coast for a while. Don't allow yourself to fall into that trap. Creating momentum when there is none is much more difficult than sustaining momentum when there is some. When you've done the hard work of creating it, leverage it.

When you are successful, you will have more energy, more confidence, more people paying attention, and more opportunities. Let's look at how you can leverage momentum in each of these areas.

When you have more energy, you will feel better. When you feel better, you're more likely to be motivated to make additional things happen. Instead of celebrating how great you feel by taking some time away from your mission, channel the energy into the next project or a new opportunity for growth. Use the energy you've gained to do something you've been putting off because you didn't feel like it. Just do it. This will leverage the energy created by momentum.

When you achieve success, you will have more confidence. Success breeds success. With a greater level of confidence, you will see things differently. Step back and consider your options for continuing to move yourself forward. Things that were not previously on your radar will suddenly appear. Use the confidence you have to stretch yourself in areas where you lacked confidence before. Move beyond your comfort zone and try something completely new. This will leverage the confidence created by momentum.

When you're making things happen, people are likely to notice. People will see you moving forward. They will be more likely to want to help you or be helped by you. Most often, both will happen. Gaining support will give you a boost. Helping others will give you a boost. When others want to help you more or be helped more because of your success, you're leveraging the visibility created by momentum.

When you're successful, people will talk about you. They will praise you. They will recommend you. Ultimately, others who believe what you believe and are interested in what you're interested in will notice you. As a result, you will have more opportunities which can lead to additional success. When you act on new opportunities because of past results, you are leveraging the opportunity created by momentum.

There's something you want to do, something you want to accomplish. Don't wait because as Karen Lamb said, *"A year from now, you will wish you had started today."*

The most successful people intentionally create momentum and never lose it. Once they get started, they never stop. They know creating momentum is like trying to roll a large heavy object such as an automobile. It takes a tremendous amount of energy to get it going, but it takes much less energy to keep it going. Your climb to the next level will be very much the same.

You may struggle at first to figure out who you want to become and where you want to be. This is often the hardest part of intentional growth, but it's necessary. Zig Ziglar said it best, *"Growth is painful. Change is painful. But, nothing is as painful as being stuck somewhere you don't belong."* However, once you're able to clearly define your vision, pay the price, and actually start moving in the right direction, you're able to continue down the path with much less effort.

Your success will not only benefit you. As you create momentum, your success will begin to positively impact the lives of those around you at home and at work. The ultimate way to leverage momentum in your own life is to help others create momentum in their lives. When you begin to intentionally impact the lives of others positively, you are maximizing momentum. It is no longer about your journey. It is about you helping others along their journey.

Achieving your own personal success must come first because you must steady yourself before you can support and lift others. There's no greater success than helping someone else become successful.

"Before you are a leader, success is all about growing yourself. When you become a leader, success is all about growing others." ~ Jack Welch

27

SUCCESS LED ME TO MORE SUCCESS

WHY WE DO WHAT WE DO DETERMINES WHAT WE GET TO DO

"Where God guides, He provides." ~ Dee Ann Turner

I believe my calling is to help others, regardless of their religious beliefs, learn to live by God's principles without quoting the scripture or referencing religion. That's why I don't share much about Christianity in my other books. I believe my mission is to help bring others closer to God by helping them improve their lives without talking directly about God. It's what other leaders did for me. And eventually, that model allowed me to find God at my own speed and in my own way. For me, if I can do that for others, I will have achieved success.

I would not have paid attention if the leadership principles had been taught to me wrapped in scripture. I would not have been interested. I would not have listened. I would not have started reading leadership books daily. I would not have found God.

My goal as I lead and influence people is not to manipulate, but rather to motivate. I know if I keep my leadership teaching neutral, I will impact and inspire more people regardless of their religious beliefs. I believe that's a worthy mission to undertake. I want to help bring others closer to God, not force them to choose God.

God gave us free will, so we could choose our own

path. He didn't choose to make others follow Him, neither will I. Jesus didn't manipulate. He motivated. He modeled leadership which influenced others to choose to follow. For me, if people are following effective leadership principles, growing their character in a positive way, becoming better people, and becoming successful in following their passion to find their purpose, I have achieved success. And, they are achieving success.

As I sit and write this book, it is early fall 2016. It's been over eight years since I started studying leadership and four years since I became intentional about my own personal transformation. This is my ninth leadership book. Ria and I have now released 14 books, with many more coming soon. Thomas Jefferson had this to say about success, *"It's wonderful how much may be done if we are always doing!"*

Many amazing things have happened in the last four years. Things I couldn't have imagined before I made the one poor choice that has led to many good choices. Today, I know God was guiding me all along. Although I didn't believe in Him, I was obviously following Him, one leadership principle at a time, to find my way home. He was leaving a trail, so I could find Him. I did.

I read something yesterday that fits perfectly here. It comes from the Bible, 2 Corinthians 5:17, *"Therefore, if anyone is in Christ, he is a new creation; old things have passed away; behold, all things have become new."* I've learned a lot more about leadership and a lot more about God since choosing to work on my character. The two continue to merge as I continue my intentional growth journey.

I learned early on that leadership is influence. Since becoming a Christian, I have been able to see the leadership principles Jesus modeled for us much more clearly than many lifelong Christians. Not because I'm better than them, but because I've been studying leadership and many of them haven't.

God created the perfect model of leadership: influence. He could have made us all follow Him. However, He chose to create the model of influence using Jesus. He was basically modeling this phrase, *"If I can't influence you to choose to follow me, I cannot lead you."* That's also the perfect model for high impact leadership in the home or the workplace.

There are thousands of timeless leadership principles which can all be traced back to the Bible. When I discovered them in 2008, they launched me like a rocket long before I chose to believe in God. As I applied them, my income nearly quadrupled by 2012. Today in 2016, my hourly rates have increased up to 228 times compared to what they were in 2008. Applying these principles led me to great success. And eventually, they led me to Him.

Leadership principles may or may not lead you to God if you haven't found Him yet. Whether you're a believer or a non-believer, aligning your actions with leadership principles will also move you toward greater success.

I've learned the truly successful among us intentionally help others achieve success. That's why my mission is to help you get to the next level and beyond.

"I'm learning more everyday that God doesn't prefer hearing what we are programmed to ask and pray for, He wants to hear and talk about what we were born for!" ~ Tonya Spence

SECTION 10

SIGNIFICANCE IS THE FOUNDATION OF LEGACY

28

SIGNIFICANCE IS THE FOUNDATION OF LEGACY

SUCCESS IS ABOUT GETTING RESULTS, SIGNIFICANCE IS ABOUT HELPING OTHERS GET RESULTS

"We build and defend not for our generation alone. We defend the foundations laid by our fathers. We build a life for generations yet unborn. We defend and we build a way of life, not for America alone, but for all mankind." ~ Franklin D. Roosevelt

Success is all about you, what you have achieved, and what you will achieve. However, to make a greater impact, you must shift your focus to significance which is all about helping others become successful. Significance is not about how far you advance yourself, significance is about how far you advance others.

The most successful people do not settle for success. They hunger for more. Not for themselves, but for others. They understand success is a stepping stone along the path toward significance. As John Maxwell observed, *"Once you have tasted significance, nothing else will satisfy you."*

With significance, what started out as a simple vision for your own personal growth has now compounded into a vision to help others achieve and succeed. You no longer must only sacrifice for yourself. Your vision is now much bigger than you. Therefore, if you want to truly experience significance, you must begin sacrificing for the benefit of others with hopes they too will someday choose a life of significance.

However, most aren't willing to sacrifice for themselves, much less others. The few who are willing to sacrifice for others will move far beyond success and live a life of significance. Those who have achieved significance will not leave a legacy for others. They will leave a legacy *in* others.

5 Signs You Have Reached Significance

(Adapted from my book, 10 Values of High Impact Leaders)

1. **You can never learn enough.** You're not focused on a formal education. There is no graduation date. You're focused on a lifetime of learning and growing. You're not concerned with the generalized knowledge the masses possess. You know your passion and have found your purpose. As a result, you are laser focused on developing highly specialized knowledge in your area of giftedness.

2. **You help others climb the ladder.** Your concern has moved beyond your own success. You're now focused on the success of others. Because you're a lifetime learner with specialized knowledge, you are uniquely positioned to help others, who value what you value, climb more efficiently and effectively up the ladder of success. You are rare! Instead of selfishly hoarding knowledge, you share it intentionally with others.

3. **You help others become wealthy.** Not only do you help others climb the ladder of success, but you also help them become more valuable. You teach them this secret: *"If you want to be a success, don't focus on*

becoming successful. Focus on becoming more valuable." You know true wealth does not mean having money. True wealth is having the ability to produce wealth.

4. **You seek growth.** You know real growth is a result of personal growth. You apply the 80/20 rule in this area. You spend 80% of your time working on areas of weakness relative to your character. You spend the other 20% of your time working on areas of strength relative to your competency. You know research studies have shown 87% of your results come from character and 13% come from competency. You know all of your growth happens outside your comfort zone.

5. **You never want to retire.** Because of your endless personal growth and highly developed specialized knowledge, you no longer have a career. You've found your calling, what you were put on this earth to do. You are in the zone and can no longer distinguish between work and play. It's all the same. You love what you do, and you look forward to doing it. Not just for now, but forever. The thought of retiring doesn't cross your mind. Instead of wondering when you can retire, you wonder how long you can keep going.

When you choose a life of significance, you've chosen to live life at a higher level. Who you are matters.

"I dare you, whoever you are, share with others the fruits of your daring. Catch a passion for helping others and a richer life will come back to you."
~ William H. Danforth

29

SIGNIFICANCE IS NOT ABOUT YOU, BUT IT STARTS WITH YOU

WHO YOU ARE ON THE INSIDE IS WHAT OTHERS EXPERIENCE ON THE OUTSIDE

"Talent is God-given. Be humble.
Fame is man-given. Be grateful.
Conceit is self-given. Be careful."
~ John Wooden

When you choose a life of significance, your life is no longer just about you and what you have accomplished. Significance is far bigger than any one individual. Significance is about touching the lives of others in a way that allows what you leave in them to flow into others. When you achieve significance, your influence is magnified by others and multiplied through others. Significance will never be about you, but significance will always start with you.

As you reflect back on what you've learned, you should now be able to see the big picture, a picture that may not have been visible as you started reading this book. However, you should be able to see the roadmap of transformation more clearly now. *I highly recommend reading this book again with the big picture in mind.*

The roadmap of transformation begins with values and ends with legacy. How far you travel down the road of transformation is up to you. Your choices will determine the distance you're able to travel and the speed you're able to travel. Ultimately, who you are will determine how far and how fast you go.

What you choose to value on the inside will reveal your character to others on the outside. In the words of Andy Stanley, *"There is no cramming for a test of character. It is always a pop quiz. You're either ready or you're not. It's the law of the harvest at work. In the moment of testing, you will reap what you have sown."* I define character as: thinking, feeling, and acting in a congruent way while making excellent moral and ethical choices based on self-evident natural laws and principles.

Mahadev Desai, Mahatma Gandhi's secretary, when asked how Gandhi could speak for hours, without notes, while mesmerizing his audiences said, *"What Gandhi thinks, what he feels, what he says, and what he does are all the same. He does not need notes. You and I, we think one thing, feel another, say a third, and do a fourth, so we need notes and files to keep track."*

Desai was describing what it means to be congruent. Gandhi walked the talk. His actions matched his words in everything he did. He was real. He was a whole person.

In all that you do, you need to not only be congruent with what comes out of your mouth, but also what comes out of your heart. You must work constantly to align your words, actions, beliefs, and values with natural laws and principles. Your ability to live in harmony with these natural laws and principles will determine the level of trust you are able to build with others along your transformational journey.

Trust is the key to influence. Influence is the key to relationships. And ultimately, relationships are the key to your success and your ability to live a life of significance. In order to build trust on the outside, you must develop your character on the inside. Whenever I think of character, I'm reminded of the words of John Luther, *"Good character is more to be praised than outstanding talent. Most talents are, to some extent, a gift. Good character, by contrast, is not given to us. We have to build it piece by piece: by thought, choice, courage, and determination."*

Every chapter in this book is filled with principles to help you build your character. Regardless, of where we are in our lives, we all have the ability to improve our character. Your character will either launch you or limit you. It will propel you along your journey or weigh you down as you try to reach and stretch your way to the next level of success on your way to significance.

Many people don't understand the word character. Henry Cloud's definition of character and integrity is simple enough, *"Character is the ability to meet the demands of reality. Integrity is the courage to meet the demands of reality."* When you can't achieve what you want to achieve, the cause can always be traced back to a character flaw.

Character doesn't simply mean good or bad. The absolute best person you know has character flaws. Having character flaws does not make you bad. Having character flaws makes you human. Character is key.

Your legacy will be defined by your character. It will be defined by what you leave behind within others. What will determine if your vision becomes your legacy? It won't be you. It will be those who felt valued by you. It will be those who were able to allow your influence to pass through them into the lives of others.

"When you do the common things in life in an uncommon way, you will command the attention of the world." ~ George Washington Carver

30

CHOOSING A LIFE OF SIGNIFICANCE

IT'S NOT ABOUT ME,
BUT IT STARTED WITH ME

"Character cannot be developed in ease and quiet.
Only through experience of trial and suffering can
the soul be strengthened, ambition inspired,
and success achieved." ~ Helen Keller

To experience true transformation, we must be willing to transform our character. There is no other way to make it happen.

I had endless character struggles in my twenties and thirties which I share about in my book, *Defining Influence: Increasing Your Influence Increases Your Options*. I seemed to struggle endlessly during those years trying to become successful at work and to become more effective at home with my family. I grew my way through it all and made many changes along the way.

However, I never truly transformed. I kept many of my bad habits and continued to make poor choices.

I remained the same on the inside as I tried to achieve different results on the outside. There was a constant internal battle taking place. In spite of all of my character flaws, I was able to achieve success and was earning hundreds of thousands of dollars each year in my consulting business. In my mind, I had achieved success. But, I hadn't considered significance.

Until I truly became successful, I could not choose

significance. I had only achieved financial success. I hadn't achieved personal success. When I made the wrong choice in May 2012, I realized I must be able to lead myself well before I deserve to lead others at all. My transformation occurred quickly once I made the decision to focus on my character and leading myself well.

At the end of 2012, I made the decision to give up my income from process improvement consulting. I didn't renew my contracts, so I could focus on transforming myself, rebuilding my brand, and shifting my business to focus only on leadership development and personal growth. I was no longer motivated by making money. I was motivated by making a difference in the lives of others.

I didn't fully realize I was moving from success to significance, but that's exactly what was happening. I was developing a passion for helping others become successful while hoping they would also choose significance in the future.

Ria was also developing the same passion. In February 2013, she went through the John Maxwell leadership certification. In June 2013, we both went to Guatemala with John and others to help train and develop over 20,000 Guatemalan leaders. It didn't matter that we had to pay all of our expenses. It wasn't about making money. We were truly making a difference in the lives of others.

We went through additional training sessions with John Maxwell, Les Brown, Nick Vujicic, and many others in 2013. Ria also resigned from her corporate job at the end of 2013. We were now both focused on living a life of significance full-time. In January 2014, Ria and I had the privilege to share the stage with Les Brown at one of his events in Los Angeles, California.

As we became more intentional, things began

happening quickly. Our growth continued to accelerate as we continued developing ourselves. In 2014, we attended more training seminars and started writing and publishing our books as we shifted more focus toward creating our leadership development brand.

Today, we are privileged to be speaking to audiences all over the country about leadership development and personal growth. We speak to all types of people in all types of businesses. We recently spoke to 80 leaders from 40 different countries. All of them were top leaders of a multi-billion dollar, global company.

That didn't happen by accident. It happened as a result of my personal transformation. Who we choose to be determines what we get to do, when we get to do it, who we get to do it with, and how much we get paid to do it.

Our choices serve as the ink we use to write our life story. You can change without transforming, but you can't transform without changing. Who do you want to be? Where do you want to be? Have you decided to make some changes? Will you transform yourself? Deciding to do it is not doing it. You must actually do it.

"I am not what happened to me,
I am what I choose to become." ~ Carl Jung

I welcome hearing how this book has influenced the way you think, how it has impacted you, and how you have used it to transform yourself. Please feel free to share your thoughts with me by email at:

Mack@MackStory.com

To order my books, audio books, and other resources, please visit: TopStoryLeadership.com or Amazon.

ABOUT THE AUTHOR

Mack's story is an amazing journey of personal and professional growth. He married Ria in 2001. He has one son, Eric, born in 1991.

After graduating high school in 1987, Mack joined the United States Marine Corps Reserve as an 0311 infantryman. Soon after, he began his 20 plus year manufacturing career. Graduating with highest honors, he earned an Executive Bachelor of Business Administration degree from Faulkner University.

Mack began his career in manufacturing in 1988 on the front lines of a large production machine shop. He eventually grew himself into upper management and found his niche in lean manufacturing and along with it, developed his passion for leadership. In 2008, he launched his own Lean Manufacturing and Leadership Development firm.

From 2005-2012, Mack led leaders and their cross-functional teams through more than 11,000 hours of process improvement, organizational change, and cultural transformation. Ria joined Mack full-time in late 2013.

In 2013, they worked with John C. Maxwell as part of an international training event focused on the Cultural Transformation in Guatemala where over 20,000 leaders were trained. They also shared the stage with internationally recognized motivational speaker Les Brown in 2014.

Mack and Ria have published nearly 20 books on personal growth and leadership development and publish more each year. In 2017, they reached 60,000 international followers on LinkedIn where they provide daily motivational, inspirational, and leadership content to people all over the world.

Clients: ATD (Association for Talent Development), Auburn University, Chevron, Chick-fil-A, EXIT Realty, Kimberly Clark, Koch Industries, Southern Company.

Mack is an inspiration for people everywhere as an example of achievement, growth, and personal development. His passion motivates and inspires people all over the world!

TOP STORY LEADERSHIP

- ✓ Keynote Speaking: Conferences, Seminars, Onsite
- ✓ Leadership Development: Leadership, Teamwork, Personal Growth, Organizational Change, Planning, Executing, Trust, Cultural Transformation, Communication, Time Management, Selling with Character, Resilience, & Relationship Building
- ✓ Blue-Collar Leadership Development
- ✓ On-site Half-day/Full-day Workshops/Seminars
- ✓ Corporate Retreats
- ✓ Women's Retreat (with Ria Story)
- ✓ Limited one-on-one coaching/mentoring
- ✓ On-site Lean Leadership Certification
- ✓ Lean Leader Leadership Development
- ✓ Become licensed to teach our content

For more information please visit:

TopStoryLeadership.com

BlueCollarLeadership.com

For daily motivation and inspiration follow us at:

LinkedIn.com/in/MackStory

LinkedIn.com/in/RiaStory

Excerpt from

Defining Influence: Increasing Your Influence Increases Your Options

In *Defining Influence*, I outline the foundational leadership principles and lessons we must learn in order to develop our character in a way that allows us to increase our influence with others. I also share many of my personal stories revealing how I got it wrong many times in the past and how I grew from front-line factory worker to become a Motivational Leadership Speaker.

INTRODUCTION

When You Increase Your Influence, You Increase Your Options.

"Leadership is influence. Nothing more. Nothing less. Everything rises and falls on leadership." ~ John C. Maxwell

Everyone is born a leader. However, everyone is not born a high impact leader.

I haven't always believed everyone is a leader. You may or may not at this point. That's okay. There is a lot to learn about leadership.

At this very moment, you may already be thinking to yourself, *"I'm not a leader."* My goal is to help you understand why everyone is a leader and to help you develop a deeper understanding of the principles of leadership and influence.

Developing a deep understanding of leadership has changed my life for the better. It has also changed the lives of my family members, friends, associates, and clients. My intention is to help you improve not only your life, but also the lives of those around you.

Until I became a student of leadership in 2008 which eventually led me to become a John Maxwell Certified Leadership Coach, Trainer, and Speaker in 2012, I did not understand leadership or realize everyone can benefit from learning the related principles.

In the past, I thought leadership was a term associated with being the boss and having formal authority over others. Those people are definitely leaders. But, I had been missing something. All of the other seven billion people on the planet are leaders too.

I say everyone is born a leader because I agree with John Maxwell, *"Leadership is Influence. Nothing more. Nothing less."* Everyone has influence. It's a fact. Therefore, everyone is a leader.

No matter your age, gender, religion, race, nationality, location, or position, everyone has influence. Whether you want to be a leader or not, you are. After reading this book, I hope you do not question whether or not you are a leader. However, I do hope you question what type of leader you are and what you need to do to increase your influence.

Everyone does not have authority, but everyone does have influence. There are plenty of examples in the world of people without authority leading people through influence alone. Actually, every one of us is an example. We have already done it. We know it is true. This principle is self-evident which means it contains its own evidence and does not need to be demonstrated or explained; it is obvious to everyone: we all have influence with others.

As I mentioned, the question to ask yourself is not, *"Am I a leader?"* The question to ask yourself is, *"What type of leader am I?"* The answer: whatever kind you choose to be. Choosing not to be a leader is not an option. As long as you live, you will have influence. You are a leader.

You started influencing your parents before you were actually born. You may have influence after your death. How? Thomas Edison still influences the world every time a light is turned on, you may do things in your life to influence others long after you're gone. Or, you may pass away with few people noticing. It depends on the choices you make.

Even when you're alone, you have influence.

The most important person you will ever influence is yourself. The degree to which you influence yourself determines the level of influence you ultimately have with others. Typically, when we are talking about leading ourselves, the word most commonly used to describe self-leadership is discipline which can be defined as giving yourself a command and following through with it. We must practice discipline daily to increase our influence with others.

"We must all suffer one of two things: the pain of discipline or the pain of regret or disappointment." ~ Jim Rohn

As I define leadership as influence, keep in mind the words leadership and influence can be interchanged anytime and anywhere. They are one and the same. Throughout this book, I'll help you remember by placing one of the words in parentheses next to the other occasionally as a reminder. They are synonyms. When you read one, think of the other.

Everything rises and falls on influence (leadership). When you share what you're learning, clearly define leadership as influence for others. They need to understand the context of what you are teaching and understand they *are* leaders (people with influence) too. If you truly want to learn and apply leadership principles, you must start teaching this material to others within 24-48 hours of learning it yourself.

You will learn the foundational principles of leadership (influence) which will help you understand the importance of the following five questions. You will be able to take effective action by growing yourself and possibly others to a higher level of leadership (influence). Everything you ever achieve, internally and externally, will be a direct result of your influence.

1. *Why* **do we influence?** – Our character determines *why* we influence. Who we are on the inside is what matters. Do we manipulate or motivate? It's all about our intent.

2. *How* **do we influence?** – Our character, combined with our competency, determines *how* we influence. Who we are and what we know combine to create our unique style of influence which determines our methods of influence.

3. *Where* **do we influence?** – Our passion and purpose determine *where* we have the greatest influence. What motivates and inspires us gives us the energy and authenticity to motivate and inspire others.

4. *Who* **do we influence?** – We influence those *who* buy-in to us. Only those valuing and seeking what we value and seek will volunteer to follow us. They give us or deny us permission to influence them based on how well we have developed our character and competency.

5. ***When* do we influence?** – We influence others *when* they want our influence. We choose when others influence us. Everyone else has the same choice. They decide when to accept or reject our influence.

The first three questions are about the choices we make as we lead (influence) ourselves and others. The last two questions deal more with the choices others will make as they decide first, *if* they will follow us, and second, *when* they will follow us. They will base their choices on *who we are* and *what we know*.

Asking these questions is important. Knowing the answers is more important. But, taking action based on the answers is most important. Cumulatively, the answers to these questions determine our leadership style and our level of influence (leadership).

On a scale of 1-10, your influence can be very low level (1) to very high level (10). But make no mistake, you *are* a leader. You *are* always on the scale. There is a positive and negative scale too. The higher on the scale you are the more effective you are. You will be at different levels with different people at different times depending on many different variables.

Someone thinking they are not a leader or someone that doesn't want to be a leader is still a leader. They will simply remain a low impact leader with low level influence getting low level results. They will likely spend much time frustrated with many areas of their life. Although they could influence a change, they choose instead to be primarily influenced by others.

What separates high impact leaders from low impact leaders? There are many things, but two primary differences are:

1) High impact leaders accept more responsibility in all areas of their lives while low impact leaders tend to blame others and transfer responsibility more often.

2) High impact leaders have more positive influence while low impact leaders tend to have more negative influence.

My passion has led me to grow into my purpose which is to help others increase their influence personally and professionally while setting and reaching their goals. I am very passionate and have great conviction. I have realized many benefits by getting better results in all areas of my life. I have improved relationships with my family members, my friends, my associates, my peers, and my clients. I have witnessed people within these same groups embrace leadership principles and reap the same benefits.

The degree to which I *live* what I teach determines my effectiveness. My goal is to learn it, live it, and *then* teach it. I had major internal struggles as I grew my way to where I am. I'm a long way from perfect, so I seek daily improvement. Too often, I see people teaching leadership but not living what they're teaching. If I teach it, I live it.

My goal is to be a better leader tomorrow than I am today. I simply must get out of my own way and lead. I must lead me effectively before I can lead others effectively, not only with acquired knowledge, but also with experience from applying and living the principles.

I'll be transparent with personal stories to help you see how I have applied leadership principles by sharing: How I've struggled. How I've learned. How I've sacrificed. And, how I've succeeded.

Go beyond highlighting or underlining key points. Take the time to write down your thoughts related to the principle. Write down what you want to change. Write down how you can apply the principle in your life. You may want to consider getting a journal to fully capture your thoughts as you progress through the chapters. What you are thinking as you read is often much more important than what you're reading.

Most importantly, do not focus your thoughts on others. Yes, they need it too. We all need it. I need it. You need it. However, if you focus outside of yourself, you are missing the very point. Your influence comes from within. Your influence rises and falls based on your choices. You have untapped and unlimited potential waiting to be released. Only you can release it.

You, like everyone else, were born a leader. Now, let's take a leadership journey together.

(If you enjoyed this Introduction to *Defining Influence*, it is available in paperback, audio, and as an eBook on Amazon.com or for a signed copy you can purchase at TopStoryLeadership.com.)

Excerpt from

10 Values of High Impact Leaders

Our values are the foundation upon which we build our character. I'll be sharing 10 values high impact leaders work to master because they know these values will have a tremendous impact on their ability to lead others well. You may be thinking, *"Aren't there more than 10 leadership values?"* Absolutely! They seem to be endless. And, they are all important. These are simply 10 key values which I have chosen to highlight.

Since leadership is very dynamic and complex, the more values you have been able to internalize and utilize synergistically together, the more effective you will be. The more influence you will have.

"High performing organizations that continuously invest in leadership development are now defining new 21st century leadership models to deal with today's gaps in their leadership pipelines and the new global business environment. These people-focused organizations have generated nearly 60% improved business growth, reported a 66% improvement in bench strength, and showed a 62% improvement in employee retention. And, our research shows that it is not enough to just spend money on leadership training, but rather to follow specific practices that drive accelerated business results." ~ Josh Bersin

Do you want to become a high impact leader?

I believe everyone is a leader, but they are leading at different levels.

I believe everyone can and should lead from *where they are.*

I believe everyone can and should make a high impact.

I believe growth doesn't just happen; we must make it happen.

I believe before you will invest in yourself you must first believe in yourself.

I believe leaders must believe in their team before they will invest in their team.

I truly believe *everything rises and falls on influence.*

There is a story of a tourist who paused for a rest in a small town in the mountains. He went over to an old man sitting on a bench in front of the only store in town and inquired, *"Friend, can you tell me something this town is noted for?"*

"Well," replied the old man, *"I don't rightly know except it's the starting point to the world. You can start here and go anywhere you want."* [1]

That's a great little story. We are all at *"the starting point"* to the world, and we *"can start here and go anywhere we want."* We can expand our influence 360° in all directions by starting in the center with ourselves.

Consider the following illustration. Imagine you are standing in the center. You can make a high impact. However, it will not happen by accident. You must become intentional. You must live with purpose while focusing on your performance as you develop your potential.

Note: Illustration and 10 Values are listed on the following pages.

Why we do what we do is about our *purpose*.

How we do what we do is about our *performance*.

What we do will determine our *potential*.

Where these three components overlap, you will achieve a
HIGH IMPACT.

10 Values of High Impact Leaders

1

THE VALUE OF VISION
Vision is the foundation of hope.
"When there's hope in the future, there's power in the present." ~ Les Brown

2

THE VALUE OF MODELING
Someone is always watching you.
"Who we are on the inside is what people see on the outside." ~ Mack Story

3

THE VALUE OF RESPONSIBILITY
When we take responsibility,
we take control.
"What is common sense is not always common practice." ~ Stephen R. Covey

4

THE VALUE OF TIMING
It matters when you do what you do.
"It's about doing the right thing for the right reason at the right time." ~ Mack Story

5

THE VALUE OF RESPECT
To be respected, we must be respectful.
"Go See, ask why, and show respect"
~ Jim Womack

6

THE VALUE OF EMPOWERMENT
Leaders gain influence by giving it to others.
"Leadership is not reserved for leaders."
~ Marcus Buckingham

7

THE VALUE OF DELEGATION
We should lead with questions instead of directions.
"Delegation 101: Delegating 'what to do,' makes you responsible. Delegating 'what to accomplish,' allows others to become responsible."
~ Mack Story

8

THE VALUE OF MULTIPLICATION
None of us is as influential as all of us.
"To add growth, lead followers. To multiply, lead leaders." ~ John C. Maxwell

9

THE VALUE OF RESULTS

Leaders like to make things happen.

"Most people fail in the getting started."
~ Maureen Falcone

10

THE VALUE OF SIGNIFICANCE

Are you going to settle for success?

"Significance is a choice that only
successful people can make."
~ Mack Story

ABOUT RIA STORY

Mack's wife, Ria, is also a motivational leadership speaker, author, and a world class coach who has a unique ability to help people develop and achieve their life and career goals, and guide them in building the habits and discipline to achieve their personal view of greatness. Ria brings a wealth of personal experience in working with clients to achieve their personal goals and aspirations in a way few coaches can.

Like many, Ria has faced adversity in life. Raised on an isolated farm in Alabama, she suffered extreme sexual abuse by her father from age 12 to 19. Desperate to escape, she left home at 19 without a job, a car, or even a high school diploma. Ria learned to be resilient, and not just survive, but thrive. (Watch her 7 minute TEDx talk at RiaStory.com/TEDx) She worked her way through school, acquiring an MBA with a 4.0 GPA, and eventually resigned from her career in the corporate world to pursue a passion for helping others achieve success.

Ria's background includes more than 10 years in healthcare administration, including several years in management, and later, Director of Compliance and Regulatory Affairs for a large healthcare organization. Ria's responsibilities included oversight of thousands of organizational policies, organizational compliance with all State and Federal regulations, and responsibility for several million dollars in Medicare appeals.

Ria co-founded Top Story Leadership, which offers leadership speaking, training, coaching, and consulting.

Ria's Story From Ashes To Beauty
by Ria Story

The unforgettable story and inspirational memoir of a young woman who was extremely sexually abused by her father from age 12 to 19 and then rejected by her mother. (Watch 7 minutes of her story in her TEDx talk at RiaStory.com/TEDx)

For the first time, Ria publicly reveals details of the extreme sexual abuse she endured growing up. 13 years after leaving home at 19, she decided to speak out about her story and encourage others to find hope and healing.

Determined to not only survive, but also thrive, Ria shares how she was able to overcome the odds and find hope and healing to Achieve Abundant Life. She shares the leadership principles she applied to find professional success, personal significance, and details how she was able to find the courage to share her story to give hope to others around the world.

Ria states, *"It would be easier for me to let this story go untold forever and simply move on with life...One of the most difficult things I've ever done is write this book. Victims of sexual assault or abuse don't want to talk because they want to avoid the social stigma and the fear of not being believed or the possibility of being blamed for something that was not their fault. My hope and prayer is someone will benefit from learning how I was able to overcome such difficult circumstances. That brings purpose to the pain and reason enough to share what I would rather have left behind forever. Our scars make us stronger."*

Available at Amazon.com in paperback, audio, and eBook. To order your signed copy, to learn more about Ria, or to book her to speak at your event, please visit: RiaStory.com/TEDx

Order books online at Amazon or RiaStory.com

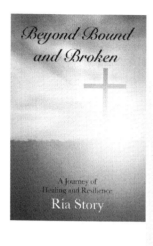

Ria Story

In *Beyond Bound and Broken*, Ria shares how she overcame the shame, fear, and doubt she developed after enduring years of extreme sexual abuse by her father. Forced to play the role of a wife and even shared with other men due to her father's perversions, Ria left home at 19 without a job, a car, or even a high-school diploma. This book also contains lessons on resilience and overcoming adversity that you can apply to your own life.

In *Ria's Story From Ashes To Beauty*, Ria tells her personal story of growing up as a victim of extreme sexual abuse from age 12 – 19, leaving home to escape, and her decision to tell her story. She shares her heart in an attempt to help others overcome their own adversity.

Order books online at Amazon or RiaStory.com

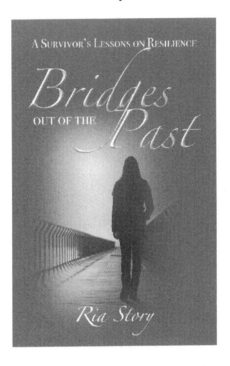

It's not what happens to you in life. It's who you become because of it. We all experience pain, grief, and loss in life. Resilience is the difference between *"I didn't die,"* and *"I learned to live again."* In this captivating book on resilience, Ria walks you through her own horrific story of more than seven years of sexual abuse by her father. She then shares how she learned not only to survive, but also to thrive in spite of her past. Learn how to overcome challenges, obstacles, and adversity in your own life by building a bridge out of the past and into the future.

(Watch 7 minutes of her story at RiaStory.com/TEDx)

Order books online at Amazon or RiaStory.com

Note: Leadership Gems is the generic, non-gender specific, version of Leadership Gems for Women. The content is very similar.

Women are naturally high level leaders because they are relationship oriented. However, it's a *"man's world"* out there and natural ability isn't enough to help you be successful as a leader. You must be intentional.

Ria packed these books with 30 leadership gems which very successful people internalize and apply. Ria has combined her years of experience in leadership roles of different organizations along with years of studying, teaching, training, and speaking on leadership to give you these 30, short and simple, yet powerful and profound, lessons to help you become very successful, regardless of whether you are in a formal leadership position or not.

Order books online at Amazon or RiaStory.com

Become inspired by this 30-day collection of daily devotions for women, where you will find practical advice on intentionally living with a grateful heart, inspirational quotes, short journaling opportunities, and scripture from God's Word on practicing gratitude.

Order books online at Amazon or RiaStory.com

Ria's *Effective Leadership Series* books are written to develop and enhance your leadership skills, while also helping you increase your abilities in areas like communication and relationships, time management, planning and execution, leading and implementing change. Look for more books in the *Effective Leadership Series*:

- *Straight Talk: The Power of Effective Communication*

- *PRIME Time: The Power of Effective Planning*

- *Change Happens: Leading Yourself and Others through Change (Co-authored by Ria & Mack Story)*

Order books online at Amazon or TopStoryLeadership.com

High impact leaders align their habits with key values in order to maximize their influence. High impact leaders intentionally grow and develop themselves in an effort to more effectively grow and develop others.

These *10 Values* are commonly understood. However, they are not always commonly practiced. These *10 Values* will help you build trust and accelerate relationship building. Those mastering these *10 Values* will be able to lead with speed as they develop 360° of influence from wherever they are.

Order books online at Amazon or TopStoryLeadership.com

Are you looking for transformation in your life? Do you want better results? Do you want stronger relationships?

In *Defining Influence*, Mack breaks down many of the principles that will allow anyone at any level to methodically and intentionally increase their positive influence.

Mack blends his personal growth journey with lessons on the principles he learned along the way. He's not telling you what he learned after years of research, but rather what he learned from years of application and transformation. Everything rises and falls on influence.

Order books online at Amazon or TopStoryLeadership.com

"Sales persuasion and influence, moving others, has changed more in the last 10 years than it has in the last 100 years. It has transitioned from buyer beware to seller beware" ~ *Daniel Pink*

So, it's no longer *"Buyer beware!"* It's *"Seller beware!"* Why? Today, the buyer has the advantage over the seller. Most often, they are holding it in their hand. It's a smart phone. They can learn everything about your product before they meet you. They can compare features and prices instantly. The major advantage you do still have is: YOU! IF they like you. IF they trust you. IF they feel you want to help them.

This book is filled with 30 short chapters providing unique insights that will give you the advantage, not over the buyer, but over your competition: those who are selling what you're selling. It will help you sell yourself.

Order books online at Amazon or BlueCollarLeadership.com

"I wish someone had given me these books 30 years ago when I started my career on the front lines. They would have changed my life then. They can change your life now." ~ Mack Story

Blue-Collar Leadership & Supervision and *Blue-Collar Leadership* are written specifically for those who lead the people on the frontlines and for those on the front lines. With 30 short, easy to read 3 page chapters, these books contain powerful, yet simple to understand leadership lessons.

Note: These two Blue-Collar Leadership books are the blue-collar version of the MAXIMIZE books and contain nearly identical content.

Down load the first 5 chapters of each book FREE at: BlueCollarLeadership.com

Order books online at Amazon or BlueCollarLeadership.com

The biggest challenge in process improvement and cultural transformation isn't identifying the problems. It's execution: implementing and sustaining the solutions.

Blue-Collar Kaizen is a resource for anyone in any position who is, or will be, leading a team through process improvement and change. Learn to engage, empower, and encourage your team for long term buy-in and sustained gains.

Mack Story has over 11,000 hours experience leading hundreds of leaders and thousands of their cross-functional kaizen team members through process improvement, organizational change, and cultural transformation. He shares lessons learned from his experience and many years of studying, teaching, and applying leadership principles.

Order books online at Amazon or TopStoryLeadership.com

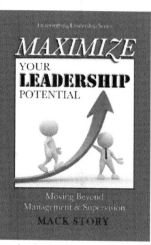

"I wish someone had given me these books 30 years ago when I started my career. They would have changed my life then. They can change your life now." ~ Mack Story

MAXIMIZE Your Potential will help you learn to lead yourself well. *MAXIMIZE Your Leadership Potential* will help you learn to lead others well. With 30 short, easy to read 3 page chapters, these books contain simple and easy to understand, yet powerful leadership lessons.

Note: These two MAXIMIZE books are the white-collar, or non-specific, version of the Blue-Collar Leadership books and contain nearly identical content.

Made in the USA
San Bernardino, CA
24 June 2018